Praise for

SOUNDTRACK

"The essays in *Soundtrack* are messages in a bottle from a time, not so long ago, when America faced down a pandemic by turning enforced isolation into an opportunity to remember the best in ourselves. They are full of grace and goodness and they remind us that when we are searching for what will save us, we need look no further than the people, the places and, yes, the songs we love. I am grateful to Alison Cupp Relyea not just for the gentle comfort her book offers but also for the fierce resolve it inspires: to live better, to love more."

—Tom Junod, two-time National Magazine Award winner and longtime friend of Fred Rogers

"With tenderness, wisdom, and a healthy dose of humor, Alison Cupp Relyea beautifully conjures the power of music to keep us grounded when the world has spun off its axis. Set in the murky heart of the pandemic, these essays vividly illuminate what happens when personal and collective history converge, showing us the world, our communities, our families, and ourselves in a new light. *Soundtrack* is a shimmering time capsule, a paean to small comforts, and a love song to the ways art can save us, again and again."

—Nicole Graev Lipson, Pushcart Prize-winning essayist and author of *Mothers and Other Fictional Characters*

"Alison Cupp Relyea blends a fan's enthusiasm and a writer's heart to show how music can help us cope with life's most challenging moments and emerge stronger than before. *Soundtrack* had me going back through the Maniacs' catalogue, proud of the influence we've had on people like her."

—Steven Gustafson, bassist, 10,000 Maniacs

"Set to the rhythm of a lifetime of music, Cupp Relyea's essays will take you by the hand and lead you through the messiest and most beautiful parts of family life. Thoughtful, poignant, and elegantly written, this is a collection to savor."

—Annabel Monaghan, bestselling author of
Nora Goes Off Script, Same Time Next Summer,
and *Does This Volvo Make My Butt Look Big?*

"As a lifelong fan of music (and great essays) as well as a mother and human being who lived through the COVID-19 pandemic, I loved Alison Cupp Relyea's *Soundtrack*. Her appreciation for the small joys during a time of sorrow (and the sorrows within times of joy) made me think, feel, and want to bust out all my favorite vinyl records."

—Janine Annett, author of
I Am "Why Do I Need Venmo?" Years Old

"By turns witty and wistful, *Soundtrack* finds unexpected harmonies amidst the dissonant chords of the early 2020s. Mixed in full effect with hopefulness, warmth, and humor, this life-affirming memoir of pandemic motherhood is best read with headphones on."

—Ari Brand, actor and playwright

"On one level, Cupp Relyea's 'mixtape' serves as a contemplative, often moving, chronicle of the covid years through the eyes of a suburban hipster mom, organized as a series of music-related vignettes. But on a deeper level, it highlights the intricate ways that songs tie into our everyday lives, often serving as the connective tissue that binds various free associations as we cobble together the fractured chunks of meaning that ground us in a big, complex world. A world made even more disorienting—and in need of synthesis—by the experience of lockdown."

—Roni Sarig, author of *The Secret History of Rock* and *Third Coast: Outkast, Timbaland, and How Hip-Hop Became a Southern Thing*

"This book is not just about music but about life—and not just about life but how music shapes and soothes the craziness of our pandemic-era existence. *Soundtrack* is a mixtape (at its core) and combines the range of emotion, writing skill, and commitment that all of us see in our favorite songs—and also in our essential books."

—Rick Burton, author of *Into the Gorge* and co-author of *Business the NHL Way*

"Alison Cupp Relyea takes the reader on a journey, seamlessly connecting her current life experiences, memories, and historical events through the magic of music."

—Melissa Montalto, musician, Funky2Death

www.mascotbooks.com

Soundtrack: Liner Notes from a Pandemic Mixtape

This memoir is a truthful recollection of actual events in the author's life. Some conversations have been recreated. The names and details of certain individuals have been removed to respect their privacy. While events in these essays have been fact-checked, some are memories, told from the author's perspective and perhaps remembered in varying detail by others.

The author referenced the *Associated Press Stylebook 2022-2024* for terms related to culture, race, and gender identity. While these conventions may change over time, efforts were made to reflect current practice and preference.

Cover design by Allison M. Fadden
Author photo by Jo Bryan Photography

For more information, please contact:
Mascot Books, an imprint of Amplify Publishing Group
620 Herndon Parkway, Suite 220
Herndon, VA 20170
info@mascotbooks.com

Library of Congress Control Number: 2023909617
CPSIA Code: PRV0723A
ISBN-13: 978-1-63755-722-8

Printed in the United States

To Rich, Rob, Eliza, and Ian—
you are my story

Hannah-

SOUNDTRACK

LINER NOTES FROM A PANDEMIC MIXTAPE

Great to make a Bank Street connection. Enjoy!

♡ ♡ ♡

20 ESSAYS
+
2 BONUS TRACKS

ALISON CUPP RELYEA

Hannah-

Glad to make a
Dark Street
connection. Enjoy!

♥♥♥

TRACK LIST

1	A BEAUTIFUL DAY IN THIS NEIGHBORHOOD	—1
2	THE EMPEROR'S NEW CLOTHES	—7
3	GOING BACK TO CALI	—11
4	I GUESS THE LORD MUST BE IN NEW YORK CITY	—17
5	THE BIGGER PICTURE	—21
6	STACY'S MOM	—31
7	A HARD RAIN'S A-GONNA FALL	—37
8	WOULD YOU RATHER?	—43
9	UNBREAKABLE KIMMY SCHMIDT THEME SONG	—49
10	DANKE SCHOEN	—55
11	SIMPLY THE BEST	—59
12	IT'S ALL COMING BACK TO ME NOW	—65
13	I'LL STAND BY YOU	—71
14	HOW YOU'VE GROWN	—77
15	DROPS OF JUPITER	—83
16	RADIO GA GA	—91
17	ZOMBIE	—97
18	ALL FOR LOVE	—103
19	GOOD RIDDANCE	—109
20	I'LL BE YOUR MIRROR	—117
BONUS TRACKS		
1	LEAVING NEW YORK	—127
2	YOU DON'T KNOW ME	—139

TRACK 1

A Beautiful Day in This Neighborhood

First, Tom Hanks got sick. Right as we locked down. That weekend, walking on the boardwalk behind Rye Playland where parts of *Big* were filmed, I listened to an interview with Hanks about his role as Fred Rogers in *A Beautiful Day in the Neighborhood*. I had recently finished listening to Ann Patchett's novel *The Dutch House*, narrated by Hanks, and it was comforting to hear his voice again. I suggested the Fred Rogers movie to my family no fewer than ten times over the next week. It was our first week of nonstop togetherness, the initial phase of what we believed to be a two-week temporary shutdown.

The first few evenings my kids outvoted me and we watched episode after episode of an odd yet strangely engaging celebrity singing show called *The Masked Singer*. Finally, I declared there would be no more voting. "Why are you so set on that movie?" my husband asked. *Because it is rare that all of us agree on what to watch. Because I love Mister Rogers. Because I just want to have something kind of certain, and a plan for movie night is something.*

When our suburban New York world shut down Friday, March 13, 2020, I was not thinking about what my stay-at-home soundtrack would be, much less that it would include the balm of Tom Hanks' speaking voice. I felt a growing instinct to reach for other voices beyond my family, some familiar and some new, to carry me, comfort me, and provide escape. In the hazy blur of unscheduled days and news reports I turned to music and stories, grateful for podcasts, movies, audio books, Alexa, and my old-fashioned record player.

My playlist was something that evolved with a couple points of origin and an unpredictable trajectory, much like coronavirus itself. It gained momentum from podcasts on long walks with our dog Mika. It provided the backdrop for the shapeless days of schooling three children from home, working from home, living through history from home—and endlessly cleaning that same home.

If asked to predict what I would listen to in a hypothetical, unimaginable, many-months lockdown, I might have assumed I would turn to the crowd-pleasing Beatles, the vulnerable poems of Leonard Cohen, or the timeless folk lyrics of Simon & Garfunkel. When I was a teenager, Simon & Garfunkel were in the part of the Venn diagram where my musical taste and that of my parents overlapped, and listening to them feels like a familiar hug. Maybe I would have guessed I would play my favorite late-night-party go-to: The Smiths. But those guesses would have all been wrong. As it turned out, my coronavirus musical recipe called for the strength of women's voices, with a timely dose of Tom Hanks. I did not choose them—they chose me.

That Hanks interview made me curious about the movie, about the decision to tell the story of Fred Rogers through his relationship with journalist Lloyd Vogel, a story inspired by a real-life friendship with Tom Junod. Hanks described the movie as an honest human lens with no sugarcoating, very much the way Fred Rogers would have wanted it: real people with real problems and flaws. I realized that while none of my three children had watched *Mister Rogers' Neighborhood*, my youngest child, Ian, hadn't even seen *Daniel Tiger*, the cartoon spin-off. At six years old, he had transitioned straight from *PAW Patrol* to whatever the older kids watched—*Full House, Scooby-Doo, Spongebob SquarePants.*

We started the movie late, with time having little meaning anymore, and the older two kids drifted off to sleep toward the end. Ian was riveted by Mister Rogers, by the characters on his show and the way he made children's television. Ian rubbed his little fists into his eyes to keep them from closing and stayed awake, waiting to find out if Lloyd's dad died, wanting to know more about all the relationships on the screen. At one moment in the film, Lloyd is driving to visit his dad while the Tracy Chapman song "The Promise" plays in the background. The lyrics and my teenage memories came flooding back as I remembered the feeling of falling in love with a song.

During college, my parents gave me concert tickets for Tracy Chapman's *New Beginning* tour in Toronto, which is where we lived at the time. It was 1996, the summer after my sophomore year, and while my best friend Laura was not a huge Tracy Chapman fan, she was there in the seat next to me at Massey Hall when the crowd waved lighters in rhythm to "The Promise." We were always together back then, when it was easier, before living in different cities and having three children each. At twenty years old, from my plush velvet seat in an old, ornate concert hall, this song told a dream-come-true romantic love story. As I listened to it now, while Lloyd traveled to visit his complicated father and Fred Rogers prayed for him, it became a song about friendship and family, a perfect love story for this imperfect moment. I pulled Ian close and held him, watching the Tom Hanks version of Fred Rogers fill my living room with compassion, devotion, and big questions in a moment when we had no answers.

The next day, we started our neighborhood project in the basement. With internet printouts of Mister Rogers' Neighborhood and The Neighborhood of Make-Believe, we descended into a small cave of toys and chaos. Armed with free time, a glue gun, cardboard boxes, and unpaired socks to make King Friday and Daniel Tiger puppets, we began to create our Rye neighborhood. Outside our house, our actual neighborhood—or rather Westchester County— quickly became one of the country's first COVID-19 hotspots. We watched updates on the news, but down there we felt safe. I played Tracy Chapman and 10,000 Maniacs on our portable speaker while Ian and I worked. He did not seem to mind that I played my favorite songs over and over again.

Ian asked questions about the lyrics, picking up on certain words in the songs as I sang along. He turned to me for help decoding Natalie Merchant's words and, hearing "Fast Car," wondered if some cars are actually faster than others. I tried to explain in a couple brief sentences before he was distracted by his art again. As a teenager, I'd wanted to know the meaning behind every song, as they held clues to a larger world. I remembered quoting Tracy Chapman in a paper about social change for a college writing seminar. I got a C on the first draft, with the comment, "This ("Talkin' Bout a Revolution") was not one of the texts I assigned. Please revise for your final draft." I removed the Tracy Chapman reference and got an A-, but what does it say about education that now, twenty-five years later, I have no memory of the other texts and only remember my "mistake"? *Mister Rogers says we learn from our mistakes,* I thought as Ian struggled to get the googly eyes to line up on his King Friday sock. His frustrated tears told me now was not the time to impart this wisdom so I said, "Let me help you," instead.

Between crafting spurts, I had to unload the dishwasher, cook, and do all the other chores that had increased tenfold because we were all home all the time. I put on episodes of *Mister Rogers* from the 1970s, and while I worked Ian watched and learned. He learned how pretzels are made, how battery-operated cars work, and how children face challenges like a parents' divorce or using a wheelchair. The characters on the show taught us to be good humans and lifelong learners, and to hold these values constant despite bumps and obstacles along the way. Mister Rogers didn't shy away from the tough topics, and since our world was suddenly turned upside down, some child-centered, purposeful perspective seemed healthy. Each time I heard the theme song as a new episode started, I felt a little closer to understanding what Fred Rogers meant by a beautiful day. There's nothing like a pandemic to teach us that while life is not all rainbows and unicorns, those single socks that never find their pair in the laundry can become magical.

TRACK 2

The Emperor's New Clothes

A week or two into New York's new state of social distancing, my friend Jenny messaged me, "Did you see this article? Good to hear she's still doing her thing!" with a link to a *Washington Post* story about Sinéad O'Connor. Eager for non-corona news, I sat at my dining room table and read the piece from beginning to end. I tuned out my three kids and let myself go to a place of deep connection with someone I've never met but who has held my hand—or my ear—through teenage angst and now in the face of a pandemic.

Jenny sent me the article because she and her husband, Matthew, had been over at our house in the summer of 2017 when Sinéad O'Connor broke down on social media from a motel room in New Jersey. They did not laugh when I got teary-eyed watching Sinéad's emotional video. Jenny, Matthew, and I played our favorite songs from *The Lion and the Cobra* and *I Do Not Want What I Haven't Got* on my orange Crosley record player, a purchase intended to

7

teach my young children about rock music and real vinyl. Sinéad's albums were among my first purchases at Clockwork Records in Hastings-on-Hudson and I played them often, but I hadn't thought in any depth about who she was as a person since I was a teenager. Jenny, Matthew, and I reminisced about what her music meant to us and how she was an unlikely yet significant role model for our generation. Reading posts from Sinéad's friends who were checking in on her, we talked about mental health and how deeply she experiences the world. A gift and an Achilles' heel at the same time.

My kids were confused by the level of interest I had in Sinéad's music. It wasn't a "Yeah, when I was growing up I loved Guns N' Roses" kind of nostalgia. As a teenager I'd felt such admiration for this young singer, not only because of her incredible voice, but because of all that she stood for. Physically beautiful but rejecting that as her image, intelligent to her core, poetic, powerful, soft, strong, outspoken, humble. She taught us about politics, religion, femininity, love, and vulnerability. She showed us that we could be something, have a purpose, that we mattered. When I was thirteen, the twenty-three-year-old Sinéad O'Connor imprinted her voice and her words in my psyche. Now I was forty-three, and the fifty-three-year-old version of her spoke to me again, more moving than ever, her decades-old songs bringing me back to who I was long ago, and shaping who I will be when we can push play again after this long worldwide pause.

Throughout March and April I kept returning to Sinéad's music to inspire my new "unloading the dishwasher" dance or "this is my only ten minutes of alone time" shower soundtrack. Sometimes I carried our Amazon Alexa with me through the house—I started calling her Lexi. I tried to remember to unplug her out of consideration for my husband Rich's fear of Big Brother, but really, with the president suggesting people inject Clorox to fight the virus, I was pretty sure no one was paying attention to us. As I wandered around with my modern-day boombox, Sinéad's voice offered an outlet for wild teenage emotions while placing me squarely in the moment of 2020, full of fear, gratitude, and overwhelming responsibility.

No song got me dancing and unloading the dishwasher faster than "The Emperor's New Clothes," and the line, "I see plenty of clothes that I like but I won't go anywhere nice for a while" could be the coronavirus tagline. No time wasted on shopping these days. Nowhere to go, no one to see. Just me, my family, some writing, my music, and an unprecedented need to dance around my house.

Sometimes in those very early days we tried to make things feel special and create family bonding experiences. We ventured out for a few hikes and completed a giant puzzle on our dining room table. On karaoke night I put on real clothes. My family cleared out of the TV room during my heartfelt rendition of "Gold Rush Brides" by 10,000 Maniacs but I didn't care. It put things in a historical context to think of westward-bound women giving birth in covered wagons long ago. Social distancing? *We got this.* I was singing for my sanity, because on any given day of the pandemic I could veer from feeling like the determined, empowered version of Sinéad from my youth, to being caught in the grips of isolation and fear, and back again. Music was the one thing that helped bring the daily roller coaster back to level ground.

Alexa kept mixing the same stuff for me over and over because my musical taste, particularly in that comfort-seeking moment, was frozen in the decade between ages thirteen and twenty-three. Sinéad, Natalie, Tracy, Patti Smith, and the occasional Cranberries,

Queen, U2, Velvet Underground or Belle and Sebastian. Pandemic Queen requests were mostly for nights when Rich and I cooked together. When "Crazy Little Thing Called Love" came on we danced in the kitchen to our wedding song.

Lockdown gave our children a crash course in infectious disease, household chores, marriage, and music from the '80s and '90s. But given that pre-pandemic dinners had consisted of the kids and me eating a rushed meal between hockey and theatre practice with Rich out of town or working late most nights, even they found some silver linings in quarantine family time. Plus, the kids find Rich and me far less embarrassing when their friends aren't around. It was just the five of us on this wagon, suspended in time and cycling through the same pairs of sweatpants.

TRACK 3

Going Back to Cali

March engulfed us in a sea of shapeless, dateless days, and as the calendar icon on the bottom of my laptop increased one day at a time, I remembered that before all this we had been planning a trip, a family vacation to California for spring break. I had text exchanges from late February with friends who lived in various California cities giving them approximate dates and checking to see if we could meet up. Once lockdown was official, I was glad I had stopped short of booking hotels and flights, saving myself the phone calls to sort out cancellations. We would have been leaving the first week in April had the concept of travel not vanished into thin air. During my daily walks along the boardwalk in my town, no planes flew overhead, no hums of their engines as they transported people to and from the New York City airports. Rich and I never spoke about California, as there was nothing to discuss. We just knew it wasn't happening. As New Yorkers we were discouraged from even venturing into bordering states, so we stayed put. We each developed our own strategies to move through the day, get our work done, and function as a family.

In those early lockdown weeks it became obvious that our baking, skateboarding, and biking skills far outperformed our ability to structure our day around remote learning and Google Classrooms. We were bumping along, keeping up with the light academic demands but only with persistent nagging and a lot of papers scattered around. The workspaces we set up were mostly abandoned as the kids appeared many times a day in the kitchen, pulled like magnets from their corners of the house. They lingered, snacked, and maybe did a little work.

By late March, that original two-week hiatus from school extended into the unknown, another reality we just knew without discussion. As the weight of it all set in, I panicked and did what so many mothers do when faced with failure in an impossible situation: I blamed myself. Then I picked myself up off the floor and vowed that tomorrow would be better, tomorrow I would get this whole thing off to a fresh start. All I needed were markers and encouraging words. The next morning I woke up, guzzled a cup of coffee, and made a schedule for Relyea Preparatory Academy. It included work periods and breaks, and meal plans and ideas for what we would do after school. Despite knowing deep down that structure was not going to be our pandemic wheelhouse, the evidence hung on the kitchen bulletin board, dated March 26, for a long time after that date as a reminder of my well-intended effort.

When I first saw color-coded distance-learning schedules popping up on people's Facebook pages around March 15, all blocked out for each kid and subject, I never clicked or downloaded, never followed the bait to Pinterest for more ideas. I resisted making comments like, "Look at you, rockin' this homeschool thing!" I had taught elementary school for many years and kept a pretty tight classroom schedule, but I had been parenting my own kids for eleven years at this point and I had no delusions that they would suddenly see me as Mary Poppins or Fräulein Maria. Too many expectations at this moment in time would only lead to battles, and the goal was not to strive for perfection—only to survive, hopefully with some level of harmony. With that in mind I tried to make a friendly and approachable schedule, not overly demanding, maybe even fun.

The homeschool schedule was not the first list or plan I made during the pandemic. On the previous Saturday morning I woke up before everyone else, and as I moved quietly through our cozy quarantine quarters, a century-old home full of artifacts and evidence of a full week of family time, I knew I couldn't clean this place alone. Instead of unloading the dishwasher, I made a checklist of chores for each of us, also with colorful Crayola markers. When the rest of the family got up, we started our weekend with a pancake breakfast and a cleaning party, our first of many in those early months. Rich cleaned the bathrooms—a gesture for which I will always be grateful—and the kids sorted socks, folded laundry, and wiped tables. It was a warm day for March so for the finale we threw open the doors for fresh air, rolled up the rug, and all three kids cleaned the hardwood floors. With buckets and bowls full of soapy water and kitchen towels, they splashed around on their hands and knees, delighting in the opportunity to make a mess in the name of cleaning.

"Ah! Bathing suits!" Ian declared, standing to get his big sister's attention and approval as the dark circles on the knees of his sweatpants expanded. Nine-year-old Eliza dashed upstairs with Ian just behind her, and they returned within minutes, dressed to hit the beach. Rob, eleven years old and hovering on the fence between childhood and adolescence, followed their lead and showed up in board shorts.

"This is so fun! It's like Annie," Eliza beamed.

"Alexa, play 'Hard Knock Life,'" I requested as they scrubbed and laughed to the music.

The cleaning party inspired me to get out the magic markers and blank paper again. I had already helped the kids muddle through Monday, Tuesday, and Wednesday, and by Thursday, it felt like the wheels were coming off. This seemed like my one chance to salvage the situation. *If it's all over Pinterest, it must work, right?* We reviewed the schedule at breakfast and I fastened it to our kitchen bulletin board with a thumbtack as they ran to different remote work locations. It hung there for less than an hour before Rob covered it with another sheet of paper. He was too lazy to find another thumbtack and stuck it right on top of my rainbow of plans. His loose-leaf sheet had only a few words and numbers, scribbled with black marker in his eleven-year-old handwriting. It held no expectations, no colorful promises or exclamation points; only the name LL Cool J, followed by a ten-digit number.

"What's this?" I asked, bewildered in spite of its simplicity, as if unfamiliar with the concept of a phone number.

"Oh, that's LL Cool J's number. He posted it and said anyone can call him anytime. You know, because of the virus. Pretty cool, right?"

"Hmph," I muttered, staring at the number, tempted on some level to dial it to see what would happen. How an '80s hip-hop star became part of my son's pandemic emotional support network, I had no idea. TikTok? Instagram? We'd activated the data plan on an old iPhone a week earlier to allow Rob to text with friends and join chats on Houseparty. This LL Cool J discovery during what was labeled 'Math Class' on the color-coded schedule did not bode well for our screentime rules. It was still March 26, we hadn't even transitioned from morning to afternoon, and already my plea for structure was overturned.

The mention of LL Cool J reminded me of the first song of his I remember knowing, "Going Back to Cali." It was on the soundtrack for the movie *Less Than Zero*, and my sister and her best friends used to sing it when we were in middle school, long before any of us had ever been to California. For the first time in weeks, I thought about our abandoned family trip to California and the many smaller plans that also evaporated.

I resisted the urge to flip back to the schedule, realizing it had served some purpose if only in its creation. It helped me organize the day, feel some sense of control, and at least I could say I tried. Changing course, I checked the kitchen for key baking ingredients, taking comfort in the one activity that served to soothe my nerves and nourish my children at the same time. I printed out a recipe my friend Paula had emailed me for her sour cream coffee cake, a treat I had tasted one time over the winter when we were still allowed to visit other people's homes. Maybe this cake is what we need right now. With all the ingredients laid out on our kitchen counter, I waited until my kids came down from their "studies" and we set to work. As usual, the younger two measured, poured, and stirred with me, while Rob joined us just in time to lick the spatula, like The Little Red Hen's friends. He watched dreamily as I poured the batter into a cake pan, then swirled a mixture of cinnamon sugar through the surface with a knife, creating a ribbon-like pattern. Setting the timer for forty-five minutes, I sent them back to their schoolwork until the timer went off. While the kids ate their first piece, still warm from the oven, I pinned Paula's recipe to the bulletin board, right over Cool J's digits, certain this would be an important ingredient in our recipe for pandemic survival.

By the time we finally reached April, I had settled into the lack of routine and clung to my recipes to get me through the overwhelming moments. I didn't need to call LL Cool J to know we would not be going back to Cali anytime soon. This was not the sweet life, but a spoonful of sugar definitely helped.

TRACK 4

I Guess the Lord Must Be in New York City

oronavirus won't last much longer, will it? It was this kind of question, along with some math problems, that filled my head some days in April. *Three meals a day for seven days for five people equals 105 meals a week. What are the numbers of new cases, hospitalizations, and deaths in New York? How can we help?* Big and small questions floated everywhere around us. *Mom, where's my mask? Will we go back to school this year?*

By late April, the curve in New York was flattening and our area hospitals were reporting fewer deaths every day. People in my suburban community had worked tirelessly to get PPE and meals to local frontline workers, and as the demand slowed, it was replaced with cautious optimism. But in the hardest hit communities, recovery will take years, and for the thousands of families who lost loved ones, there's no such thing. New York, the city I had called home for sixteen years, was a shell of what it had been; with empty trains, shuttered stores, darkened theatres, quiet concert halls, vacant playgrounds, and basketball hoops with no backboards so people wouldn't play together and spread the virus.

I missed New York more than ever, and as bad as the disease was in March and April, I felt like a traitor, a fair-weather friend who had taken the city for granted and left before she needed me most. We tried the seven p.m. claps and calls from our porches in the suburbs, my kids with their brass instruments from elementary school band blaring into a carless, tree-lined street. It was sincere but spotty and disorganized, and I longed to lean out of an apartment window and yell over the fire escapes, bonding in anonymity with faceless neighbors.

Then, just when I needed someone to understand my mix of sadness and gratitude shining through as the storm clouds cleared, Alexa surprised me. Getting ready for a shower, I gave a typical directive: "Play Sinéad O'Connor songs mixed." A light, airy tune filled the room. Despite Alexa's reassuring habit of repeating the directions back to me, I thought she had made a mistake. The song reminded me of an upbeat '70s tune, almost Carpenters-like in its melody, yet I recognized Sinéad's signature Irish lilt telling the story of a city—New York City—with the Lord watching over it and a young woman who had spent her life dreaming of it. *Repeat! Alexa, please repeat!* I begged her, listening more closely to catch the title and lyrics.

The next morning before my children woke up, I researched this song while playing different versions on YouTube. "I Guess the Lord Must Be in New York City" was written and performed by Harry Nilsson, whose name was unfamiliar to me, though I now realized I had known his music for decades. With his song "Coconut" featured in the movie *Reservoir Dogs*, Harry Nilsson was part of the soundtrack from my college days, and now, twenty-five years later, he's part of my pandemic with his beautiful tribute to New York City.

Wikipedia informed me that Sinéad O'Connor performed her version of "I Guess the Lord Must Be in New York City" for the *You've Got Mail* soundtrack. There he was again—Tom Hanks—this time interwoven with Sinéad O'Connor and Nora Ephron. Nora Ephron was a brilliant storyteller, leaving a library of love stories, humor, and small-world coincidence as her legacy. Realizing I never saw *You've Got Mail* in 1998 because at twenty-two years old I was too cool for that kind of rom-com, I added it to my list. Maybe my kids would watch it with me, or maybe they would pick *The Masked Singer* again and I'd get some alone time.

To quote The Sundays, "Here's where the story ends." At least in my mind, when I started writing down these memories and turning them into an essay in early May, that's where it ended. This writing was supposed to be "that little souvenir from a terrible year that makes my eyes feel sore." Something for my kids and me to wistfully read years from now, all wrapped up with a happy song and New York on the upswing. Tom Hanks had recovered, Sinéad was home in Ireland, New York's curve was flattening, and my family and I were doing okay, taking it one day at a time and heading into warmer months hopeful that we were trending toward normalcy. Then some things happened that made me wonder, *What is normal, anyway?*

TRACK 5

The Bigger Picture

"I love your hair!" a new acquaintance said to me at elementary school pickup, not long after we moved from New York City to Rye in 2014. I could tell she was referring to my grey streaks, most pronounced near my temples but beginning to send out soldiers to other parts of my hair with increased persistence.

"Thank you," I answered with a smile before turning my gaze back to the stairs, watching for my son's kindergarten teacher to arrive with her procession of five- and six-year-olds.

"Such courage," I heard the woman then say. I turned to see where she was looking, wondering what courageous event was unfolding here at pickup, only to find her still looking at my hair.

"Oh, thanks."

The teachers and kids tumbled out the door, and the moment passed with my feelings left unspoken, but later that day and many times afterward I thought about this interaction and what it said about the town where we now lived. Being a white thirty-something woman with greying hair in a community where many people my age either were not yet going grey or chose to dye their hair was something that simply happened, not a courageous decision or a daring act. In fact, it would have taken more motivation and time to go to a salon and change my appearance.

As we settled into schools and activities that first year, I was beginning to understand my new surroundings and what felt at times like a collegiate conformity. Car brands, home decor, and children's activities fit into certain molds, and on more than one occasion, the answer to a question I asked was, "That's just how we do things here."

In the years since then, mostly through my work in education at the local historical society, I have learned more about how Rye has fostered a level of homogeneity: from a history of housing discrimination to municipal border decisions that carved separate communities out of one larger town. I lived near Playland Parkway, a common place for traffic stops, and it seemed the majority of drivers stopped by the police were not white, despite the town having a population that is roughly ninety percent white. In late May 2020 the grey-haired memory resurfaced as questions of race, stereotypes, and power unseated the health-related pandemic questions.

On May 25, three days before our country hit 100,000 covid deaths, George Floyd was murdered. It was Memorial Day. For a few months now the mantra had been, "We're all in this together," a feel-good saying that glossed over the mounting political tension. We were spending the holiday weekend at a beach with close friends, a family from down the street who had become our pandemic pod. In various combinations of kids, adults, and dogs, we went for walks, played games, and cooked meals together, the change of scenery and ongoing discussion providing space to reflect. Even a task as mundane as going to the grocery store was part of a larger story. At this crucial intersection, the reality of who was hit hardest by the virus, the inequities of the past and present, and the slanted stories in history books were thrust to the forefront.

I grappled with how to answer my kids' questions and how much to read on social media late at night or before sunrise. The factual questions were easy; the 'why' questions were more challenging. I reminded myself that it's okay to say, "I don't know." It's not as though this murder was the first of its kind, not even the first to make national headlines in the past few months. Ahmaud Arbery was killed in February 2020, and Breonna Taylor on March 13, just as the covid walls went up. By May, held in this moment of relative stillness, George Floyd's death reverberated around the country. It didn't matter that Minneapolis was far away from where we lived. Our phones and laptops were windows looking out to the world. As we absorbed this event, one Sinéad O'Connor song kept playing in my head: "Black Boys on Mopeds."

I'd been singing this song at various moments throughout the pandemic, mostly alone while folding laundry or on the infrequent car rides to run masked errands. When I had started listening to Sinéad again on my record player a few years earlier, every word came back to me from my Walkman days. "Black Boys on Mopeds" is about two victims of police brutality, and thirty years after the album's release—thanks to the internet completing my research—I know their names, too: Colin Roach and Nicholas Bramble. While still in that rabbit hole of curiosity, I found a 1991 *Rolling Stone* interview with Sinéad. She described systemic racism and its impact on the music industry long before it was a term in my vocabulary, stating:

They [the media] don't want people to think for themselves. The only way that people are getting the opportunity
to think for themselves at this moment is through music.

And in particular, the hip-hop movement, which is why
the censors are doing their fucking level best to stop it. It's
complete racism. I would have been censored if it wasn't.
Loads of people would be. Madonna would be. Madonna's
records got to Number One. Vanilla Ice – let me make this
point, "Ice Ice Baby" is a complete rip-off lyrically of N.W.A.
and loads of people.

Sinéad's music always had an undeniable relevance that carried
it beyond its origin in 1980s England. Now, I found in it a question
or an unfinished lesson: *If history keeps repeating itself, what can we
do to change its course?*

On my walks in the weeks that followed I listened to podcasts. I
had a lot of learning to do, and from many more relevant sources than
a song by a white woman from decades earlier. Rob and I first heard
about George Floyd's roots in the Houston hip-hop scene through an
episode of *The Daily* podcast called "I Want to Touch the World." The
tragedy of George Floyd's death was only one layer of his life story.
On my own, I listened to a podcast called *Seeing White*, a fourteen-part
series from *Scene On Radio*, which gave historical context to racial
identity. But all of this is not the same as taking action.

Talking to my kids was also not enough. It was better than not
engaging, but it came with the privilege of choosing when and how
we have discussions. On July 16, 2019, when Attorney General
William Barr ordered that the Eric Garner case be dropped, I was
listening to the coverage with Rob—ten years old at the time—while

picking up Eliza from camp. It was Eliza's ninth birthday. When she got in the car, I reached to turn the knob to adjust the radio to another station, but Rob asked to keep listening. We listened.

Rob and I filled Eliza in on the case. As the words "I can't breathe" echoed out of the car speaker, she did not ask me to turn it off. Rob surprised me with details I had not shared with him, like Garner's age and occupation. Mr. Garner worked for the New York City Department of Parks & Recreation. He helped take care of parks and playgrounds like the ones where my children spent afternoons playing as toddlers. "All because of cigarettes?" Eliza asked. I don't regret having that conversation with my kids, but talking about race and injustice in a suburban parking lot does little to dismantle the structures that lead to these events. I could see that now.

I thought back to my own childhood in Malvern, Pennsylvania, also a small town with little diversity where stereotypes flourished, and challenges to those stereotypes made a lasting impact. Dr. Levi Wingard was the principal of our high school at the time, and one of only a few Black educators in the district. Students approached him with admiration, respect, and with a little bit of fear we might end up in his office—exactly how one should feel about a high school principal. Dr. Wingard was known for his tall stature and strong voice, but what I remember most was his deep faith in young people, and not only the rule-followers and top students. Now, thirty years later, I thought about what it meant for my Black classmates to have that mirror in leadership and wondered what kind of obstacles or racism Dr. Wingard may have faced from the school community.

Outside of school, I had my MTV and role models like Sinéad. When I was lucky enough to catch her on TV, I studied Sinéad O'Connor, head shaved, body cloaked in shapeless fabric, lyrics powerful, voice clear. Unlike me, she was making an intentional statement with her hair as well as her lyrics. Sinéad criticized Margaret Thatcher and sang of Black boys on mopeds, a story unfamiliar to me, as were many of her references. Sinéad used her music to advocate for others and identify sources of oppression, and the importance of that went beyond the history lessons in the songs. While her actions invited critics and sometimes came at a cost to her career, they also deepened discourse and led people to confront difficult topics.

My writing and teaching at the Rye Historical Society is a very, very small stage from which to speak, but there are—I've discovered over the years—stories worth telling that can contribute to a more complete and complex understanding of our community. Of course, we have the famous tales (and diary entries) from when George Washington stayed at the Square House, the historic house museum where my colleagues and I work. That's a fine story, but by nature of having grown up in Malvern, only a few miles from Valley Forge, it was hard to go for a bike ride without passing a house where George Washington once slept. I didn't need to tell his story, especially the glossed-over version often taught in schools. It was much more interesting to find local heroes, those not represented in textbooks, and share their stories. After George Floyd's murder, as my inbox filled with statements of solidarity from every consumer brand or nonprofit that had ever collected my e-mail, I wondered how our town would mark this moment in history.

The nationwide fight for racial justice intensified in early June as activists and allies filled streets and parks across the country. Locally, two young women, Amanda and Cristiana, accomplished something unprecedented in Rye. On that same stretch of Boston

Post Road that George Washington traveled on horseback, about a thousand people gathered in a March for Justice on Saturday, June 13. Amanda and Cristiana were two recent college graduates, both also graduates of the local high school, and they teamed up with other young people and leaders to plan the program and the march. I left the house that day with eleven-year-old Rob, eager to attend his first march and hopefully see some long-lost classmates. We had no signs or T-shirts—which I suddenly regretted—but out the door we went, walking the mile to downtown.

After all that time isolating, the energy and shared purpose of the crowd was exhilarating. First, they held a Speak Out on the Village Green featuring members of our community—young activists, elected officials, leaders of the NAACP—who shared their insights on issues that matter both nationwide and locally. And we listened to ways our decisions have an impact. *The ballot box! The bookstores! The box office! Yes, yes, and yes!*

When the speeches ended and we marched through the streets, it was the faces and voices I remember most, some familiar but most new. Any age, race, grey hair, black hair, blond hair, blue hair, no hair—we all marched together.

Some people came from neighboring towns and were probably on their fourth or fifth march since Memorial Day; others I recognized from school pickups and soccer sidelines, and they had probably never marched before. And here they were. Voices joined together in chants, and one of my favorite memories was walking alongside someone who led a chant. I listened as the words, first spoken by only one voice, caught on in surrounding layers of people and grew louder with each repetition.

The March for Justice felt like a sea change in our town, a place where putting up lawn signs had been somewhat taboo in pre-pandemic days. People told their life story in car magnets instead. By May, there were graduation signs on lawns for every kid moving from one school building to another. Then "Love Rye" signs appeared, and "Thank You Frontline Workers" signs, and even an occasional "Hate Has No Home Here." People were coming out of their houses again, maybe a little weary, but also more aware. On that June day, they were ready to listen.

From Amanda and Cristiana I learned about the obstacles they encountered in planning the march, from being told they needed multi-million dollar insurance coverage to navigating ambiguous covid guidelines. At every turn the first answer they got to most requests was "no." Soon they found allies in leadership who shared their goals and believed in them. They were given support and encouraged to rely on a centuries-old constitutional right: the right to peaceful assembly. Rather than sitting at home letting my hair go grey and worrying about the world, I could take my kid out to follow their lead. Marches may be criticized as performative, but that doesn't mean they are not important. It is hard to quantify the impact of an event that lasts a few fleeting hours, but one of those speakers, Jamaal Bowman, went on to get elected in November 2020, becoming the first Black congressman to represent Rye.

After leaving the march, a piece of that unity and shared responsibility came home with us, and probably with most people in the crowd. In those early summer days, Rob played hip-hop songs by his favorite artists, like Lil Baby's "The Bigger Picture," written to capture the weight of this moment. Through playlists, news media, friends, family, teachers, and TikTok videos, Rob was piecing together the truths of American history, finding role models and heroes, and developing his own covid soundtrack. I wonder what will stick with him in thirty years.

TRACK 6

Stacy's Mom

On a hot summer afternoon, I flopped on the couch with a new book, hungry to actually read something from start to finish. The unstructured early pandemic months could have been a great time to read, but my attention span, like so many other things, was completely off balance. I resorted to reading pseudonews articles, likely with a low retention rate. By July though, I was ready for Rebecca Makkai's *The Great Believers*. It was an escape to read good fiction, but the strong parallels to our current moment in history left me reeling with memories. As I peered through the author's fictional window to lives destroyed or forever altered by AIDS, the reality of a different pandemic, one we had lived through yet never fully processed, sunk in.

The last play I saw before the pandemic was about AIDS and family. On a surprisingly pleasant January day, I met a few friends near Union Square in New York City and we saw Ari Brand's *Scenes from Childhood*, a play about a man whose father died when he was a child. The man finds out as a young adult that the true cause of his father's death was AIDS. For a few weeks after seeing the play, before the word coronavirus had even entered our vocabulary, I spent a lot of time thinking about other lives cut short by AIDS, and all those families unmoored in the wake of tragedy.

I guess I was talking about it too, because my kids started asking questions about the AIDS pandemic, curious about this era from before they were born. It came up the way September 11th does, with small, specific questions that, over time, lead to a more complete picture. With HIV and AIDS, the world did not stop for years, or months, or even a day. Childhood in my small Pennsylvania town didn't change in tangible ways, yet we felt a growing sense of fear and anxiety about things that already made many of the adults around us anxious and fearful—sex, drugs, and the life-altering consequences of adolescent choices. Through my teenage years, HIV/AIDS was a cloud hovering over us, tangled up with the coming-of-age things my friends and I were supposed to find exciting. Shrouded in fear, it was best left undiscussed.

When my friend's mother got very sick the illness was inexplicable, and all we knew, even as kids, was that she might not live. When she died, her cause of death, as with Ari's dad, was called something else—cancer, lymphoma, pneumonia, chronic illness. None of us knew it was HIV until many years later. Before she was sick for so long, she baked cookies and made us hot chocolate after we went sledding down the small hill in their yard that seemed as big as a mountain. She was a mother and a wife; a teacher, neighbor, and friend. In the '80s and early '90s a bubble of silence, shame, and confusion enveloped the disease, keeping it hidden just out of reach, even in those moments when it hit close to home. We watched it shatter worlds around us, but without a name, it remained elusive and abstract. It happened in my town, it happened in the playwright's family, and it happened in every corner of our country.

And yet, sometimes it felt like it didn't happen at all. When March 2020 arrived and first China, then Italy, and now our metro area were on twenty-four-hour news cycles I hardly heard any mention of the HIV/AIDS pandemic. Nor did I think about it much myself in the face of this new immediate threat. As the weeks passed, someone would occasionally mention it when we measured the lengths between pandemics, or labeled past generations by their defining disease. In the news, most references were to earlier points in history: the 1918 influenza pandemic, the development time for the polio vaccine. Anthony Fauci had a long history in HIV/AIDS research, and when stigmas and healthcare inequities emerged around COVID-19, some news stories mentioned parallels to HIV/AIDS. But most of the time we stayed in the moment, staring at line graphs and investing in sanitizer. It felt like control and was easier that way.

By July though, I had time to reflect and read and imagine, and pain from the past could be interwoven with the present. On early mornings with the summer sun rising through my living room window, I read *The Great Believers* before the house woke up, walking in the shoes of fictional characters and connecting to the stories from my youth again. Deaths measured in numbers, dates, and locations don't hit as hard as stories of families, love, and desperate loneliness.

We were fortunate to not suffer any family deaths from covid, but my kids remember Tom Hanks being sick and our relief that he recovered. They remember the evening in early April when we played the song "Stacy's Mom" over and over again in honor of Adam Schlesinger from Fountains of Wayne. I even let them watch the highly inappropriate music video on YouTube. *What the hell? We're in a pandemic.* Then John Prine died, and Wynton Marsalis's dad, and the guy who wrote "I Love Rock 'N Roll." I played some Joan Jett that day while making dinner. These lives and the thousands of others were not only numbers and statistics. They too were parents, spouses, siblings and friends; artists, musicians, and writers.

While I read the novel, I sometimes played "Stacy's Mom" again, mixed in with Queen in memory of Freddie Mercury. I scanned my shelf for my old copy of Patti Smith's *Just Kids*, looking for the photographs of a young Robert Mapplethorpe frozen in time. Who else? I tried to remember. Arthur Ashe. Rock Hudson. I Googled Eazy-E, conjuring up the lyrics of N.W.A.'s "Gangsta Gangsta," a song a few of my middle school friends used to quote with very little understanding of its meaning. My thoughts drifted away from the public eye to Ari's dad and my childhood friend's mom. When *Philadelphia* came out in 1993, I had just moved from Pennsylvania to Toronto. I watched the movie with my new neighborhood friends at a church youth group one wintry Sunday night. My friend's mom had died five years earlier, and in that time the world was finally getting ready to grieve more openly. And there he was inviting us in with a story to tell: a younger Tom Hanks. It was a sign of the times that a big-name straight actor was cast as a gay character in this intimate portrayal, but regardless of that, the film helped confront the pain of the disease. People had been dying from AIDS for over twelve years by then.

What happened to God's Love We Deliver? I wondered, an

organization where I volunteered in 1998 while at my first post-college job in Gap's corporate offices.

I pictured my twenty-two-year-old self heading out during my lunch hour, holding a list of addresses and prepackaged meals in brown paper bags, each one marked for a homebound person living with HIV/AIDS in the Chelsea neighborhood near my office. Over twenty years later I still recall the sounds of buzzers and doorbells, shuffling slippered feet, and the tile floors of the hallways in the historic London Terrace apartment complex and smaller buildings along West 23rd Street. We exchanged so few words, passing a bag from my hand to theirs, and I remember wondering if there was more I should say in these moments. (By the way, as of this book's publication, God's Love We Deliver is still delivering meals to New Yorkers with chronic illnesses, working harder than ever through this recent pandemic.)

These diseases made me think of the clichéd expression, *the tip of an iceberg*. The names of people we know, both due to their fame or because they touch us personally, float in a thin layer above the surface, the visible shell of an enormous collective. One morning in early July, as I checked texts and news alerts before sinking into my book, a headline flashed: Broadway actor Nick Cordero dies at forty-one after a long battle with COVID-19. Broadway and all its fans, quiet for four months now, awakened with a collective mourning for one of their own. Our country had cheered for Nick, and now his wife Amanda and their little son joined the other families dealing with tragedy. The show would someday go on, but with missing pieces, broken hearts, and shadows on stage.

TRACK 7

A Hard Rain's A-Gonna Fall

rior to the summer of 2020, I hadn't considered activism to be a character trait of our suburban town, yet a week after the March for Justice, a crowd gathered again for a Pride Month celebration on the Village Green. Youth leaders gave inspiring speeches while young children made rainbow-themed crafts and played beneath the trees.

To close the ceremony, three siblings performed the Indigo Girls song "Closer to Fine." I've known every word to that song since I was fifteen years old yet hadn't fully processed the way its meaning connects to identity. While not specifically about LGBTQ+ identities, the message of young people finding themselves fit the moment. Even adults are a work in progress.

The line that I always heard loudest when I was younger was "Help me take my life less seriously." My mom used to—and still does—remind me to laugh and not be too hard on myself. I need that voice in my head suggesting that questions often have more than one answer, especially now that I'm a mom of kids on the brink of adolescence. Searching for the right way is a waste of time.

I thought I had outgrown the Indigo Girls, but no, I still loved this music and how it transported me to teenage memories. I remembered listening to the album *Rites of Passage* while lying on a rocky lake in Canada with high school friends during our last pre-college summer.

We looked up at the millions of stars and wondered where our lives would go from there as "Galileo" played in the background. Was that the Milky Way we saw? We thought so. In college, it seemed that every guy who played the guitar knew "Closer to Fine," as if it were part of a Top Ten list of tips for appearing deep and romantic. It always made me laugh a little, but I found myself singing along.

After the Pride celebration, the Indigo Girls made their way onto my Pandemic Soundtrack, and my daughter Eliza requested their music in the car. "I like the Smith siblings' version better," she proclaimed the first time she heard the original. Eliza asked if the Indigo Girls were gay. Earlier she had asked me if there were any pictures of Sinéad when she had hair, and why she had shaved her head. Over the months, Eliza started developing an understanding of the links between appearance, expression, and identity, and these musicians gave us a way to find answers to her questions. It also meant we got to listen to good music while we talked.

The rest of the summer felt quiet, despite the country moving toward a presidential election that fall. Pandemic school drew closer and occupied the main stage of worries and political tension. The normal excitement of September was overshadowed by words like "hybrid learning" and "protocols," and the first weeks of school were weird. There is no other good way to describe it. We were all on a whole new learning curve, and the goal was to get through each day preserving enough energy to face the next. I stayed in my little world until big moments pulled me out.

For me, the first big event that fall was the death of Ruth Bader Ginsburg. I didn't cry right away. I had a mix of emotions similar to when my grandparents died in their nineties—sadness along with gratitude for the full life she lived and a curiosity to learn more. It was anticipated yet devastating, complicated in what it meant for our country. One of our biggest defenders of civil rights, the archetype of the term "small but mighty," was no longer in place to uphold the laws she and others fought so hard to establish.

A few nights later, awake and alone in the middle of the night, I played one of my favorite videos on YouTube. It was the first song I listened to that brought me to tears after Justice Ginsburg's death: Patti Smith's version of Bob Dylan's "A Hard Rain's A-Gonna Fall" at the Nobel Prize in Literature ceremony. It was a formal, fancy event with an elegant audience of kings and queens, princes and princesses. Patti Smith is many things, but fancy is not one of them.

A couple of minutes into the song, she faltered mid-line and paused. She apologized, tried to continue the line, faltered again, tried to pick up the next line, then stopped singing completely. Turning to the musicians behind her with a small smile, her eyes full of feeling, she said, "I'm sorry. Can we restart that part?" Then, to the audience, "I apologize, I'm so nervous." People applauded in support (or most of them, anyway). She resumed singing, and made it through to the end.

I'll never know what I find more beautiful—the incredible grace and vulnerability with which Patti handled that moment with that audience, or the fact that it happened against the backdrop of those lyrics. "A Hard Rain's A-Gonna Fall" is a journey through the world, through the senses, and through the human psyche. A funeral song of despair for sure, but of love and beauty, too.

Watching Patti in front of that audience reminded me of the petite RBG standing up for what's right in Capitol Hill, surrounded by people who don't look like her and some who likely preferred not to listen to her. She proved herself with strength, courage, conviction, humility, and humor. She showed that fitting the mold is not as important as blazing a trail. Justice Ruth Bader Ginsburg among the suited majority-male judges and politicians in Washington was a lot like Patti on that stage, singing on bravely after asking to begin again, her long gray hair and lack of makeup conspicuous amongst the tuxedos and gowns and diamonds.

Oh, how I wished throughout these last many months, these last years, that, like Patti Smith, we could restart this part or that part, do it over again. I have dreamed that our country and our world had some do-overs, like a children's game of kickball where the players can't agree if the runner is safe or out. "Do over!" they call, and everyone knows to get back to their previous spot. Instead, we have to carry these words, these women, and their lives forward with a vow to do better for the next generation.

One of my favorite lines in "A Hard Rain's A-Gonna Fall" is, "I met a young girl, she gave me a rainbow." It screams, *Life has all gone to shit but there's still beauty and joy and hope. There's still a reason to keep going.* I see my daughter in that line, her love of music and her love of life. The day after my midnight Nobel Prize viewing, I overheard Eliza singing "Closer to Fine" and I smiled at that little sliver of legacy, a memory that only happened because, within the push and pull of politics, we'd marked a moment with music months earlier.

The next day, Eliza made a plan to bring a picnic breakfast to a nearby park and watch the sunrise. I woke her up and she toasted waffles and filled a small Tupperware container with syrup. She packed forks and plates and napkins in her fabric lunch bag, and we put on our shoes and light jackets and walked out into the crisp fall air. I played music as we walked the two blocks to the park, then we settled in on a bench overlooking the water and opened our breakfast. We listened to Indigo Girls and Patti Smith's cover of Bob Dylan as we ate waffles on paper plates, watching another day begin. We didn't have all the answers and there were no do-overs, but at that moment, we were a little bit closer to fine.

TRACK 8

Would You Rather?

Early in the covid pandemic, while on a Zoom call with my extended family, my husband Rich proposed we play a game of Would You Rather? aimed at my slightly germaphobic and reclusive older brother, Sam. He is the one person I know who felt quite comfortable with covid restrictions from the very beginning, as he would have happily embraced masks and social distancing ages ago if it were socially acceptable. Sam is also a scientist, so his responses were analytical and represented the scientific findings related to COVID-19. It went something like this:

Would you rather lick a New York City subway pole or use a public bathroom? Sam has never been on a New York City subway and avoids public bathrooms under normal circumstances, so this was a very hypothetical situation. His answer was that given that the virus seemed airborne and not something one could ingest, he would wear a mask, then hold his breath and lick the pole quickly rather than flush a toilet or be in close quarters with other toilet-flushing, potentially-ill people. The game was endless and covered nearly every aspect of public health and regular life—masks, sanitizer, indoors, outdoors, airplanes, trains, restaurants, social distancing, hugging, and handshaking.

Months later, in October, we spontaneously started a new round of the game, involving only Rich, the three kids, and me. We were having family dinner for the millionth night in a row. One of my New Year's resolutions on January 1, 2020 had been, "More family dinners—and we should plan menus and cook together!" I had pictured us being on teams, the entrée team and the dessert team, once a week—a way to reconnect amid our busy schedules. We successfully accomplished one ambitious family dinner before the pandemic and I remember feeling grateful for the togetherness. By October, the novelty of family dinners had worn off, but we were all still there, taking the same seats at the table every night.

The menu that night was steak because Rich read somewhere that zinc is good for fighting the virus, and we had a kid in quarantine for two weeks because of close contact at a hockey game. Covid felt as close to home as it ever had, seven months in. *Or eight? Are we at eight months yet? Who knows.* We ate steak and vegetables and crossed our fingers that Rob would skate by this time uninfected.

For some reason, Ian was always at the head of the table for dinner these days, despite being the youngest. He was still young enough that he barely stayed in his seat, and the game started with him asking our Alexa to play a couple of different kinds of farts on the Fart Sounds app he had purchased months earlier. The other kids jumped in, and their attempts to be grosser than one another quickly morphed into Would You Rather? It gave them the opportunity to be totally, creatively disgusting, and they built on one another's ideas. Unfortunately for me, we were only in round two or three when someone had the nerve to insult not only me, but my now all-time favorite singer:

"Would you rather be locked in a closet for twenty-four hours or listen to Sinéad O'Connor songs for twenty-four hours?" *What?!?!* I couldn't believe it. Did they have no appreciation for the musical education I'd been imparting? Everyone who has ever been a kid knows what to do when a mom expresses dismay or hurt as the butt of a family joke—double down and repeat. I complimented my husband on the steak and tried to play it cool, reminding them to put napkins on their laps and that they were more than capable of getting their own waters. Nothing worked to distract them, and with Alexa playing the role of fourth sibling, I was outnumbered. They stood up from their seats, each trying to one-up the last contestant.

"Would you rather listen to Sinéad O'Connor or plunge a toilet full of poop?" "Would you rather listen to the song 'WAP' over and over or Sinéad O'Connor?" I couldn't help but laugh. *Alexa, please don't play that "WAP" song at dinner,* I thought. They went through Taylor Swift, then a high-pitched, energetic children's artist Ian loves named Parry Gripp, Roddy Ricch's "The Box," and other music intended to inspire the response, "Please sing the clean version!"

Then all three kids started singing "I Guess the Lord Must Be in New York City" in mocking voices, watching themselves in the mirror next to our kitchen table as they danced with exaggerated movements. Eliza swung her hips from side to side in time with the music and picked up her little brother to swing him around while Rob made goofy smiling faces in the mirror, eyes wide and eyebrows raised. Alexa responded by playing the original version of the song, and Rich and I each picked up a kid and swung them around.

As they danced and teased me, I asked, "Would you rather listen to the Sinéad O'Connor version or the Harry Nilsson version?" Sinéad, they answered. At least she beat some competition in the game, although many people would argue for Nilsson's original. We all sat back at the table to eat our cold steak and I savored this moment that never would have happened were it not for our strange new world.

Would You Rather? feels like the ultimate sibling game. It's a game best played with people who know each other well, often when they are stuck with one another and have little else to do. It starts with nothing and ends with gut-splitting laughter, requiring only a creative mind, a sense of humor, and a context that lends itself to idle time, like a road trip, a camping trip, or a power outage. As my kids' game dissolved into a dance party and then into bedtime, I thought about my own siblings playing the game months earlier as adults, and how lucky I am to have my three siblings in my life. And their spouses, children, and dogs.

Sometime over the summer, I had heard a song called "Would You Rather" and I wondered about it, trying to recall the artist. *Phoebe Bridgers*, Google answered. Yes, I had played Phoebe Bridgers one day on a walk after discovering her music. I listened to the song again, surprised and not at all surprised to realize it was about Phoebe and her brother. It's about what it means to have a sibling, what we inherit when we move through life with these people, assigned and not chosen, arranged in an order that no one can control and that will forever shape us. Siblings are tethered to us. They share our story and know what we know in a way that no one else can, and when we look at each other, we see the person today layered with snapshots from years of yesterdays. We cherish them and can't stand them, but cannot imagine life without them.

I missed my adult siblings, never having gone this long of a stretch without seeing them, while my own children were constantly together and could not turn a corner in our home without bumping into one another. The chorus in Phoebe Bridgers's song, "I'm a can on a string, you're on the end," pulls me right back to childhood: making those "phones" out of Dixie cups and string and sharing secrets with my siblings that we would never tell our parents. As kids, we crowded on our family room couch watching TV and movies, kneeled next to each other close to the screen playing Atari, smashed in together on the bench seats in the back of the station wagon, and jiggled the locked doorknob of our one shared bathroom in the morning before school.

Through all the months of the pandemic, my siblings were there for me any time I called, holding the can on the other end of the string. It amazed me how long we could stay on the phone, often not saying much at all. Rich used to joke that at any given moment, there were likely two Cupps on the phone with each other somewhere in the world.

When my kids won't stop arguing or say the meanest things to each other, when I want to crawl into a closet and scream for them all to stop, I have to remind myself that all those pushes and pulls are part of tightening the string. Would you rather your kids sit still at the dinner table or get up and dance together? I'll take the dancing every time.

TRACK 9

Unbreakable Kimmy Schmidt Theme Song

The scariest part of Halloween was, by far, the moment I tore my calf muscle. It was a typical forty-something injury, caused by almost nothing. Halloween had already been rough. Only a few hours earlier, I broke the news to Eliza and Ian that they would not be able to do the covid-safe, pre-packaged, spaced apart on a card table, highly sanitized grab-n-go Halloween trick-or-treating organized by the neighborhood. We were still waiting on PCR test results for Rob from a hockey team exposure. Ian cried in a mid-afternoon bath, asking if we were going to have Thanksgiving or Christmas or anything good this year. He could see by my expression that I could make no promises and sobbed a little more as the news sunk in. Ian was growing tired of the changes, and he wanted to see his grandparents and cousins and have his regular childhood again. His seven-year-old tears over missed celebrations and monotony dissolved in the hot water, bubbles, and lavender-scented Epsom salt. He laid down in the water with just his face and knees showing above the bubbles and closed his eyes.

When Ian emerged dripping in his towel, he had absorbed the trick-or-treating news with resilience and had ideas about how we could do Halloween at home instead. He was used to this by now. A half hour later, as we planned a replacement indoor party, I opened my email to negative PCR results, a delightful twist for two eager trick-or-treaters, happy to carry an extra pillowcase to fill with treats and leave outside their quarantined older brother's door.

Rich, Eliza, and Ian braved the outdoor world with costumes, masks, and bags, ready for the one-hour extravaganza of socially distanced sugar collection. Rob stayed in his room while I blasted some Hamilton songs and ran around the house putting away two giant loads of laundry, opening the windows as I moved through the rooms, energized by the crisp fall air. This was the rollercoaster. Each day the mood could darken and lighten multiple times with very little actual change in circumstances. "We have to always be ready to pivot," I'd recently heard someone say.

Then, right in the middle of the song "You'll Be Back" by the King George character, I pivoted too quickly rounding a corner to get another stack of freshly-folded laundry. A pop, audible in my memory, took my right leg out and knocked the wind out of me. I hobbled first to the freezer for an ice pack and then to the couch, where I FaceTimed Rob, still in his bedroom. He hung up on me the first time, apparently because he was on Houseparty with his friends and thought it was a mistake. Believable. The second time he answered, and I begged, "Call Dad. Please." Trick-or-treating was scheduled for a very brief hour, and Rich and the kids were already on their way home.

The one thing I did only for myself those first many months of the pandemic was take my daily walks. The walk along the boardwalk in the morning with the dog, the walk through the nature preserve in the afternoon without her. These were my lifelines. I had even started running a bit over the past month. Just as covid cases in our area were quickly on the rise again and every large publication in the US was reporting story after story of mothers who were bearing most of the brunt of this new world order, my one source of emotional balance slipped away, at least temporarily. Googling 'torn calf muscles' and texting a friend who had recovered from the same injury, it didn't look as bad as I first thought. A week of no walking, maybe two more of limited distances, and then no running for a while.

After my leg had mostly healed and I had a special brace to wear, I started to pay attention to an object in my bedroom that I had previously ignored on good days, resented on others, and employed as a drying rack now and then—the Peloton. Rich had bought the bike a couple years earlier to help a recurring back problem. While I should have been excited, I have always preferred exercising outside to any sort of instructor-led class or stationary machine. For a couple of years I quietly refused to even try on the shoes he ordered in my size. Now, unable to go for long walks, I shuffled over to the machine to take a closer look. I found the main power button and saw that someone had already set up a profile for me, although I was stuck when it asked for a password. By this point in the pandemic, seeing the words "Reset your password?" on a screen gave me a quick jolt of anxiety. Login screens with their many passwords linking us to assignments, meetings, and websites had become a disproportionately large part of our life.

Back on the home screen, I clicked on my daughter's profile and found I could get right in. Slipping on those strange Velcro clip-in shoes like a slightly terrified Cinderella, I prepared to spin in place on this fancy overpriced bike complete with sweaty, enthusiastic instructors rumored to have amazing playlists. When I got to the screen to choose my class, I couldn't do it. This form of online learning remained a bridge too far for me. I hear that people find the encouragement from the instructors motivating, the challenging sprints a goal to achieve. I am not one of those people, and I was not ready for this Peloton pressure.

Then, as I sat uncomfortably on the pointy seat, an unfamiliar choice caught my eye: Scenic Rides. That I could handle. Now this machine became kind of like an airplane, and after months of no travel, I clicked on faraway places where friends and family live, or where I've always wanted to go, and off I rode. Wellington, New Zealand. Melbourne, Australia. Santiago, Chile. All in thirty minutes or less. At some point early in the pandemic, I'd seen people's posts about taking virtual tours of the Louvre and the Taj Mahal. The idea seemed lovely, but I hadn't embraced couch travel. Now, with my busted calf muscle, I had to do something, so I biked around the world, a glass of ice water with lemon resting on my dresser, my 1980s women singing in the background. Anytime Kate Bush's "Running Up That Hill" came into the mix I pedaled a little faster through the rainforests of Costa Rica or along the canals in Venice.

For a couple weeks I was content with this, and then I had the great idea to set up Ian's at-home learning center on our bedroom rug, a couple yards from the Peloton. The learning center consisted of a math workbook, a folder, a bowl of baby carrots, a cup of water and a pencil. He thought it was kind of novel at first, and we could finish most of his at-home learning within a thirty-minute workout. Soon he grew frustrated that I couldn't see the math problems or instructions and he had to read them to me to ask for help. Plus, this level of multitasking, though efficient, was cutting into my alone time. Ian had a full three hours to do his work each morning. We could multitask at other times, like lunch, so out the door he went.

At the same time, the biking trips around the world were not quite enough anymore. No matter where I went virtually, the scene outside my bedroom window revealed short, cold New York December days and here I was, strapped into a stationary bike. Without the scents of the ocean or the markets, without the feel of gravel paths beneath my bike tires or the sounds of birds and street noise, two-dimensional travel lacked all the sensory delight of real travel. It was impossible to forget I was staring at a screen and pedaling to nowhere. *Now what?*

The answer was *Unbreakable Kimmy Schmidt*. A good friend of mine wrote for the show, and while I had watched a couple episodes when it first aired, my kids and work had been getting in the way of me watching much television for the past dozen or so years. The Netflix trend, like the Peloton, was lost on me until the pandemic. So Kimmy and I climbed out of our bunkers and joined the rest of society together. I set up a laptop on the handlebars and rode, escaping my home in the suburbs to travel to Kimmy's basement apartment in the fictional Upper New York neighborhood of East Dogmouth.

The clever writing had me laughing immediately, and while the exaggerated premise—a young Midwestern woman escapes a cult leader's bunker and lands in New York City—had little in common with our current predicament, it resonated. Kimmy's kindness was contagious, and her can-do attitude had me approaching the challenging winter days with a little more humor. During the opening credits and theme music, someone from Kimmy's hometown comments, "Females are strong as hell!" It made me think of all the women who were holding families together, trying to hold on to their jobs, checking in on older relatives, monitoring their children's at-home learning and doing the majority of the regular household stuff at the same time.

In this pandemic, as in every time period to-date, most of the teachers in our public schools, the school nurses tracking down daily health forms, and the caregivers in healthcare settings were women. Many of them were also the emotional backbone of their families. Major media outlets were highlighting stories of women who found themselves in impossible circumstances, alongside statistics measuring the impact the pandemic has had on their jobs, childcare, families and overall well-being. *We are strong as hell and now it is winter and we are tired. We are tired of worrying, tired of snacks, tired of trying to keep all the balls in the air and tired of silver linings.*

Kimmy always found the silver linings, and she taught the hilarious cast of characters around her to see the glass half full, even in the most preposterous of situations. Whether it was the show's life lessons or the healing power of laughter and sweat, I treasured this escape. It was hard not to regain a sense of optimism, and even as I was able to go out for long walks again, I kept hopping on the bike to ride alongside Kimmy and see life through her rose-colored glasses. I pedaled a little faster when the short, punchy theme song came on, a reminder that a woman's strength goes beyond muscles and speed. Someday we would leave our pandemic bunkers behind and start our own fascinating transition—hopefully on real bikes exploring new places in a vibrant, multisensory world. Until then, East Dogmouth was good enough for me.

TRACK 10

Danke Schoen

Huddled in for a pandemic winter with calendars now reading 2021, our world was still a sea of change and tension set against the mundane tasks of dishes, laundry, bedtime stories, and reminders to bring gloves to school, even if one did not want to wear them. It was January, the coldest month of the year, but also the month of fresh starts and new opportunities. Joe Biden, proving there is such a thing as a second, third, or fourth chance, was inaugurated as president, with Kamala Harris breaking through glass ceilings and marking numerous first-times as vice president. Even if it felt long overdue, it felt good. And there on stage at the Lincoln Memorial and on televisions across the country was the man whose reassuring words kicked off this soundtrack: Tom Hanks.

I called Ian back in from skateboarding to see his now-favorite actor and listen to musical acts both familiar and new, and the other kids also came out of their hiding spots to watch. All five of us crowded onto a blue/green couch that should have been replaced years ago and had by now folded under the pressure to provide around-the-clock comfort. Its sunken cushions were beyond repair, molded into the shape of our family after ten long months. Drinks, yogurt, or who knows what spilled over the years had left stain marks on the arms of the couch. The dog licking a certain spot usually indicated a new spill, and I rarely challenged her cleaning skills with my own.

When Tom Hanks announced the next musical act, I asked from my submerged middle couch spot, "Who are the Black Pumas?"

Panning to the stage, a man who seemed to have heard my question replied, "Hello. We're the Black Pumas from Austin, Texas." My children exploded in laughter, and another family story was born. I learned that Eric Burton was the lead singer, and the band had been nominated for a Grammy in 2020 for Best New Artist. Had I been living in a hole? Well, sort of. A few minutes later, we replayed Amanda Gorman's "The Hill We Climb," a poetic time capsule and salve for our wounds. We headed to bed after the inauguration, hoping poetry and new leadership would help unify our broken country. The vulnerability of our nation in the wake of the January 6 attack was palpable, even through a television screen.

By morning, one person emerged with the unique power to unite, at least on social media, and that person was Bernie Sanders. The multiplying collection of Bernie memes with his mail and hand-made mittens had their own Instagram accounts and were featured in the opening of every late-night show. Rob and I looked at some of our favorites together that evening, laughing as we tried to one-up each other in our searches for the best Bernies. As he headed up the stairs to bed, he casually mentioned that he liked Sinéad O'Connor now. "Why?" I turned and asked.

"Oh, cuz I guess she was one of the artists Lil Wayne saw on TV a lot when he was young and yeah, he gives her a shout-out in one of his songs." Yes, Lil Wayne, the rapper pardoned by Trump a few days before he left the Oval Office, changed Rob's opinion of Sinéad in a thirty-second TikTok video. I Googled and confirmed the story and the song, "Ball Hard." It played on my computer as I wrote this essay. I never would have predicted Rob's change of heart, but could I have predicted much of anything during coronavirus? Life may always unfold in random, unexpected ways, but never before did I have so much time to sit on my couch and observe it so closely.

To quote a character we studied in-depth during the pandemic, "Life moves pretty fast. You don't stop and look around once in a while, you could miss it." Ten months into covid, Ferris Bueller's words did not feel so true. Life was slow and strange and messy. Big cities like Bueller's Chicago were quiet, his Chicago Cubs had no live fans, and he and his best friend could never have snuck the sports car out of the garage because their parents would be working from home upstairs. Cutting school for fun was a distant memory—the Ferris of the pandemic would have been begging to go to school, eager to see his friends again.

Yet, during one of our countless movie nights, 1980s Ferris took my kids on outrageous adventures and they learned the song "Danke Schoen," laughing as he sang in the shower and on a parade float. I wondered, *Where did all those years go?* How did I now have kids so close in age to Ferris, Cameron, and Sloan? I was ten years old when I saw that movie, the same age Eliza was now.

Switching from Lil Wayne to "Danke Schoen," I thought about how as much as we try to reject our parents' musical preferences, they often seep through. Rob's little nod to Sinéad added a drop of glue to what binds us. I wondered about the history of "Danke Schoen," realizing that if it hadn't been on a movie soundtrack, I may never have heard the song, despite it being popular when my parents were teens. I learned that it is the Pennsylvania Dutch pronunciation that allows for the clever rhyming with "pain" and "explain." While Wayne Newton's melodic voice came through my computer speaker, my thoughts wandered to my German grandmother, from whom I learned other Pennsylvania Dutch sayings, like putting the word "awhile" at the end of a sentence. "You kids go get dressed for dinner. I'll set the table awhile." She turned one hundred in June of 2020, a life bookended by pandemics. We were supposed to have a big party with a band playing music from her life's soundtrack, but the details were quickly whittled away to nothing. We replaced the party with covid-safe photographs, letters, and phone calls, and I didn't see her for more than a year.

At some point during the pandemic, I saw a bumper sticker on a pickup truck that read, "Where am I going, and why am I in this handbasket?" I nearly choked on laughter, then got teary-eyed remembering my grandmother's voice when she chided us as kids with her favorite saying. In place of being able to see my mother and grandmother, I held close the handmade treasures they gifted us through the years—quilts, cross-stitched samplers, holiday ornaments and knitted winter accessories. Maybe this was why everyone loved Bernie's homespun mittens so much. Covid gave new meaning to "hell in a handbasket," yet in spite of all the worry, tension, and pain it caused, small moments kept poking through, reminding us to say danke schoen.

TRACK II

Simply the Best

Early in the pandemic, around April or May, I'd taken a friend's recommendation and started watching *Schitt's Creek*. I love Eugene Levy and it was exactly the comedic escape I needed. I watched it before dawn while my husband and kids were asleep. I would turn it off as soon as I heard footsteps, allowing little moments of the Rose family's absurdity to pop into my head throughout the day, a source of laughter when our reality seemed, well, just so shitty. I'd watched about two seasons before getting distracted. Summer had arrived, remote school had "let out," and I added the show to my mental list of pandemic projects I'd started but never finished.

Fast forward to winter 2021. We were seasoned navigators of the pandemic by now and we rented a house in The Berkshires for a ski vacation, our first true change of scenery in nearly a year. Eliza and I were exploring the area on our first day when we found the cutest little gift shop in Egremont. The store was filled with rainbows and humor, and on a table near the checkout counter Eliza spotted the unofficial *Schitt's Creek* coloring book. "That's the show you liked, Mom. You should get it," she said when she saw it. I bought it as a gift to both of us along with some colored pencils, and she quickly set to work back at our rental house, coloring in the iconic *Schitt's Creek* sign on the first page.

The kids spent about a half hour that evening asking what was so funny about *Schitt's Creek* and begging to watch it. Since we were on a vacation and I had recently glanced at an article about the merits of watching this show with your kids, I said yes. I had only really read the headline, but in my fuzzy memory of the pre-dawn episodes from the first two seasons, it wasn't too off-color. Plus, I might finally finish something!

Little did I realize how much we could learn from the Roses as we approached the one-year mark of COVID-19. The new terms we'd adopted—*social distancing, pod, quaranteam*—had become depressingly familiar, even oppressive. There was still no end in sight, no widely available vaccine, no certainty about anything. And then there they were, just when we needed them: Eugene Levy and Catherine O'Hara playing parents in their sixties with two grown children, all holed up together in two adjoining hotel rooms, leaning on one another, driving each other crazy, getting to know the meaning of family, and facing a new reality with a sense of humor.

My kids became obsessed by the end of the first season. Eliza loved Alexis, Ian kept rewinding to see David's facial expressions again, and all of us laughed hysterically at Roland and the cast of small-town characters. With a full week ahead of us, we settled into a routine of lazy breakfasts, often in the company of our new TV friends, followed by skiing and lunch outdoors at the mountain.

I went for a walk every morning before everyone was up, listening to podcasts while exploring country roads that wound through snow-covered pastures sprinkled with cows. Each day after skiing, the kids picked up where we'd left off with the show while Rich and I made dinner, catching some of the antics from the open kitchen.

This glorious break from daily life under corona continued until about noon on Wednesday. Many families we knew had encountered a rock-bottom covid moment, when something—maybe related to the disease, or maybe a typical life setback made more unsettling by the pandemic—triggered a downward spiral. For us, it was an actual downward spiral. Eliza, always a big fan of pushing herself to new heights on the slopes, hit a big jump in the terrain park with her usual enthusiasm but crashed the landing. I cannot speak to the details beyond this because only Rob was there to see it, along with a snowboard instructor who stayed with her while Rob went down the mountain to get ski patrol. To that young man at Catamount Mountain Resort who stayed close to my child while she howled in pain, thank you.

In the first aid station the medical team helped us remove her boot and stabilize her leg. Our house was only a few minutes from the mountain and we stopped there before going to the ER to gauge how serious it was. Sometimes kids bounce right back, and maybe she'd be skiing again by the end of the week! For an hour or so, I lived that dream while Eliza lay on the couch icing her right leg and smiling, if not laughing, at *Schitt's Creek*. When the endorphins wore off and the pain became more severe, Rich took Eliza to the emergency room and I adjusted my expectations—still cautiously optimistic—until he called and said, among other things I don't remember, the words "fractured tibia." Like the quick demise of the

Rose family fortune, our picture-perfect Berkshire vacation ended on that jump.

The next twenty-four hours were a whirlwind of online recommendations from moms in my town. A winter storm was approaching, and some doctors' offices had already decided to close or limit hours. Blocking any thoughts of fresh snow on the mountain should the storm come as predicted, I made phone calls, returned texts, and worked through logistics. Thanks to this network of moms, one of whom is also an orthopedist, by Thursday afternoon I had two appointments for Friday, just in case. I spent the rest of the day filling out pre-visit and insurance authorization forms and helping Eliza hobble to and from the bathroom, careful not to bump her cardboard and ACE bandage-wrapped leg.

Friday morning, I settled Eliza on the couch to watch *Schitt's Creek* and still got out to walk and talk to the cows. Digging deep for gratitude that the injury and the snow storm were not worse, I focused on the day ahead and walked through the steps. We'd drive into the city to the Hospital for Special Surgery, get casted, discuss treatment, and make it back that night. Start early. Move slowly. Drive carefully.

Back at the house after my walk, I downloaded some books on Audible: young adult titles I looked forward to sharing with my daughter. I settled Eliza in the car, her leg stabilized by pillows and blankets, a snow boot on one foot and a sock on the other, the seatbelt wrapped around her little body at an odd angle so she could recline in the back seat. I tossed the crutches, her new silver accessory, into the trunk. We drove past the cows, their brown and cream bodies looking bright against a fresh sheet of white snow, as the narrator introduced our first book, Jacqueline Woodson's memoir of her early life, *Brown Girl Dreaming*.

For those hours, Eliza and I were transported to another life, the story of another mother and daughter with problems, heartache, love, and joy of their own. We escaped into the story as light snow speckled the windshield and open country roads shifted to highways and then city. We had to pause the book when we arrived at the hospital where things went smoothly, Eliza's pain having subsided by this point. With a toe-to-hip cast on her right leg, and a pink Starbucks drink clutched in her hand, we settled back into the Volvo to finish the story while heading north to the mountains.

As Jackie, which Woodson was called as a child, grows up and her struggles move from within the family to Civil Rights activism, Eliza and I paused to talk about our country's history, and what we are still dealing with today. In spring of that year, Eliza would study the Civil Rights movement. I wondered what she would remember about Jackie—her family in Brooklyn, the teacher who changed her life, family visits to the south, listening to "Love Train" by the O'Jays on the bus ride to visit her uncle in prison? Did seeing life's challenges through the eyes of another ten-year-old help Eliza in the same way that the moms sharing stories of broken bones had reassured me two days earlier?

When the book ended, Eliza reminded me of my promise to stop for fast food. She looked calm in the rearview mirror, tired from the long day and content with french fries. She leaned her head against the window and stretched her casted leg out across the backseat. Once night settled in and the roads became winding and remote again, Eliza fell asleep. I scrolled through radio stations, just in time to catch the beginning of "Love Train" on an upstate oldies station. Sometimes the world knows just what we need. With my little girl dreaming in the back seat, I sang out loud to one song after another until I passed the cows and pulled into the driveway.

The next day, we alternated between a trip to the mountain for a few final runs in the fresh powder and staying at home with Eliza, watching *Schitt's Creek* and playing card games. Ian, who had been following David's antics with a strong sense of kinship since the first season, ran to find me when David and Patrick got engaged. "They're proposed!" Ian shouted. He wore a huge smile as he pulled me by the arm into the TV room. I danced along to the couple's theme song, Tina Turner's version of "Simply the Best."

Ian and I sat opposite Eliza on the sectional and I thought for a moment about how she'd watched the first couple of seasons, her ten-year-old body in constant motion between splits, back bends, and TikTok dances while she laughed at and with the Roses. Her casted body was still now, her lower half covered in blankets, her face smiling with the same love and joy as earlier that week. This vacation had been far from perfect. It hadn't even met my adjusted pandemic vision of perfect. But it was, in a Schitty way, simply the best.

TRACK 12

It's All Coming Back to Me Now

I was lying in bed one night in late March when Susannah, a good friend from college, sent a group of us a soon-to-be-released version of a commercial she'd been working on for Orbit gum. She sent it because the eight of us hadn't seen each other in so long and soon we could, and because she had put so much time into it, and maybe to get a little feedback. I clicked the link and was transported to a post-pandemic world set against a jarringly familiar song I couldn't identify. I seemed to know most of the words somehow, slightly out of order or just a little off, and I definitely knew the powerful crescendos.

More moving, though, was the imagery. Pizza boxes, long beards, kids in the background on Zoom, and people reuniting after many months. The ad had all kinds of pandemic humor and tons of humanity and love. At first I was slightly confused, but by the end I was ugly crying and laughing alone in my bed. I played it a second time, laughing and crying again even though I knew where it was going. Susannah texted something like, "Song is still TBD, so this is a very rough cut. Please don't share." I couldn't decide how I felt about the song. I went to bed without responding.

A few days later, on the Friday evening before spring break, I sat in my living room getting organized for a long road trip. My kids were in the den watching one of those tween Nickelodeon or Disney shows where I mix up all the characters, if I try to follow along at all. A song emanated from the television and I jolted upright. "If I kiss you like this, and if you whisper like that, it was lost long ago but it's all coming back to me." It was the song from the gum commercial.

I ran into the room and demanded, "What's this show? Who is that singing?"

"Um, it's called *Country Comfort* and it's our new favorite! That's the mom," Eliza answered. As I watched this Disney mom singing karaoke on screen, a name popped into my head: Celine Dion. That's who sings the song! The title, "It's All Coming Back to Me Now," made perfect sense for Susannah's ad. After singing along to the chorus, I grabbed my home phone and called her. She answered right away, probably wondering why I would be calling on a Friday night from the landline.

"Sus, the song is perfect," I said without even a hello. She'd thought it might be some sort of emergency. I was so glad she answered, so she could feel the strength of my conviction. Once we stopped laughing, we caught up on the phone for the first time in months. Eliza asked to see the commercial, and then we watched the original Celine video before bed, a tragic love story set in a stormy, windswept castle, strange but unforgettable. Eliza loved it.

The next morning as I packed before the sun was up and ran

through my to-do list to get ready for our road trip, the song kept echoing in my head. I would never have expected a Celine Dion song to be on my Covid Soundtrack. She had never been on any soundtrack of mine—no mixtape, no vinyl album, definitely no poster on my bedroom wall as a teenager. The closest I had come to being a fan was learning all the words to the theme song from *Titanic*, and I blame that more on radio DJs and life before streaming than on my musical taste. But now I sang her song out loud, all alone, running around the house gathering books and chargers and packing a bag of snacks for the kids, giving in to its power. The power of Celine Dion.

Life was coming back to us. We were embarking on a family road trip because, not quite ready to fly, we were happy to drive somewhere new, somewhere we could explore and have adventures and make memories. I chose our destination, Jekyll Island, Georgia, with all covid considerations in mind. Our hotel room had its own entrance, and the whole island is always relatively unpopulated. It has a fascinating history and wide, long, empty beaches.

As we drove down I-95, navigating traffic, dining roadside with compliments of the Golden Arches, and stopping for bathroom breaks with three children whose bladders always seemed terribly out of sync, memories from my childhood surfaced in bits and pieces. We started the license plate game in New Jersey and by Virginia had over thirty states. No member of my childhood family had my husband's competitive streak. He and Eliza stared out their windows, laser-focused on neighboring cars, instructing me to get a little closer to the car in the next lane and squealing with delight if it filled in a gap in the list.

When I was a kid, my family did this drive every year for about six or seven years in a row. We spent spring breaks in a small town called Eustis in Lake County, Florida, an hour or so from Orlando. And with four kids, flying was out of the question. My aunt and uncle had a horse farm with a racetrack and a lake set on endless wooded acres. My sister Chrissy and I drove around the property in a golf cart, feeling the freedom of the open road long before we were old enough to drive legally. We stretched out on a grassy hill watching the horses, tanning our legs in the hot central Florida sun and running our fingers through the Spanish moss we collected from the paths below the enormous canopy of trees. We had a Sony Walkman with a double jack for headphones, and on one of our last visits to the farm we memorized the words to Suzanne Vega's "Luka."

I remember these vacations from photographs and souvenirs, and each year the journey had been as memorable as the destination. Now here I was, at forty-four years old, undertaking the same journey with my own children. *It is all coming back to me.* Everything—the car games, the Waffle House signs towering above I-95, the Beltway traffic and the songs on the radio—was seemingly unchanged, other than my placement in the driver's seat. Like my parents, I still had no good answer to the questions, "Are we there yet?" or "How much longer?"

One of the greatest highlights came, of course, when we crossed the border from North Carolina into South Carolina, after following Pedro's journey on billboards for over a hundred miles. South of the Border was everything I remembered—a glorified truck stop with warehouses of fireworks and a huge gift shop full of overpriced Mexican-inspired souvenirs. Sombrero-clad Pedro, the mascot, stood at least six stories above the attractions and motels. Our kids ran masked into the gift shop and found multiple must-haves between the front door and the bathroom. They happily blew much of their souvenir money before even reaching Georgia. I had wondered if South of the Border might have become more culturally sensitive since 1985, but no, it was exactly the same.

We arrived in Georgia and settled into the cute beachfront motel with almost no plans. Every morning I walked on the beach before the sun was up, and every night we watched episodes of *Impractical Jokers* on a network called truTV. Rob remembered when the Impractical Jokers went to South of the Border on their way to Miami, and I remembered, not with pride but with some nostalgia, that the Impractical Jokers' movie was the last one we had seen in a theatre. Would we ever have movie theatre popcorn again? It was too early to tell.

The week on Jekyll Island was simple, with bike rides and beach time filling our days. We had nowhere to go other than a skate park or a boat trip. A bike path ran along the island from our hotel to town, and we rode back and forth a few times a day, with Rob on his skateboard, Ian on his rollerblades, and Rich and I on bikes with Eliza in a cart behind one of us. Her leg was still healing from the break in February, but with her new boot she started to get her mobility back. I watched from the balcony outside our room as she and Rich played catch on the lawn one day. Her broken leg created an empty space with no dance, ice hockey, or soccer, and that week she decided to fill it with softball.

As the week came to an end, we worked our way back north in our overpacked car in desperate need of a top carrier. The kids counted down the hours, eager to see friends and get back to in-person school. We flew past South of the Border and waved to Pedro. No one asked to stop. We are a family that endures road trips. We are a family that sticks together. We are a family that is ready to go home. *It was so long ago, but it's all coming back.* Finally.

TRACK 13

I'll Stand by You

For the whole first year of covid, I had been searching for a way to make sense of this moment in history. When it had first begun, I'd started exploring old documents at the Rye Historical Society where I work, to piece together pandemic experiences from previous generations. Digging through the archives, one of the artifacts that grounded me in those early weeks was the Record Book of the Health Officer. Dating from 1923-1938, it recorded the names, ages, occupations, and outcomes associated with every single case of infectious disease in the community. Most of those diseases are all but gone from our lives today: measles, mumps, rubella, chicken pox, diphtheria, scarlet fever, pneumonia, over and over again, page after page, some pages with only one or two diseases listed because of town-wide outbreaks. Our archivist told me there was an earlier volume of the record book, one that spanned from 1910-1923 and held information about the Spanish flu, but we were unable to locate it.

My own family's past held a piece of that history. My grandmother, born in 1920 at the tail end of the flu pandemic, had turned one hundred in June of 2020, during the intense first spring of covid. Now she was approaching her 101st birthday.

We planned to celebrate her centennial-plus-one in person. It would be the first time I'd get to see her in eighteen months, though we'd talked regularly throughout the pandemic. In our phone calls she lamented her lack of freedom to see friends for dinner, card games, and book clubs, very similar to the freedoms I too missed. "We can't live like this forever," she said on more than one occasion. We were all very much aware that, at one hundred years old, she might not outlast this state of isolation, so forever was a real possibility for her.

Sometimes when I called my grandmother to catch up, I uncovered pieces of our family history. She told me that my great-great-grandfather had died from influenza in 1920, during the third wave of that pandemic. I had never even heard this relative mentioned, but now, a time in history we'd barely touched on in high school had increased in significance for me.

Living through history doesn't always feel historic, and most days are marked by only small family events that don't register on any sort of timeline, personal or global. Some days, though, we are aware of the historical import of what we're doing. On Friday, May 21, 2021, I watched Rob, then twelve, get vaccinated in his school gymnasium. Instead of sepia-tinted images or discolored newspaper articles from the 1950s depicting children in line for the polio vaccine, it was my kid in a hoodie, waiting in lines and chairs, always at least six feet from other students and parents. It was the kind of day where you think, *If someone had told me a year and a half ago what I would be doing right now, I would not have believed it possible.*

Waiting the mandatory twenty minutes post-shot, I studied the masked faces of other students and parents and noted the organized and efficient demeanor of the many health care professionals from White Plains Hospital, ushering student/parent pairs from check-in to curtain to chair. It was an incredible thing, really, to be part of this. It was the first day that our public school district was offering vaccines for students twelve and up, and only the second time I had been inside the school the entire year. The families whispering to one another, the healthcare workers moving children from station to station, and the greetings of friends reuniting created a strange crescendo of quiet, with everyone trying not to make too much noise.

I saw some of my son's friends from elementary school, children I hadn't seen since our very rushed drive-through fifth grade graduation the previous spring. I saw my friend Daniel and thought back to a night out in the city in spring of 2019 when he and I took our reluctant spouses to Times Square to see Morrissey on Broadway. How strange our world had become that concerts were now forbidden, and we gathered instead for public inoculations.

The vaccination appointment was in the middle of my work day, and during Rob's lunch break. He went off to Spanish class with barely a goodbye. I headed back to the historical society, making a note to add today to the timeline my high school interns were building. They were creating an exhibit showing how our town had responded to covid, featuring an interactive timeline that started back in February 2020. Even as they worked, some of the memories we uncovered felt blurry and distant. That initial shock, when fear of an unknown disease had collided with a two-week school closure, now felt emotionally out of reach. What had seemed extraordinary became ordinary, and as the timeline stretched into months and beyond, we were blanketed by a collective numbness.

While I appreciated the historical gravity of my kid getting the covid vaccine, the emotional weight didn't hit me until the next day, while I was listening to music and cleaning the kitchen. Hot steam billowed from the just-finished dishwasher as a familiar voice radiated from the countertop speaker:

> I'll stand by you
> I'll stand by you
> Won't let nobody hurt you
> I'll stand by you

I used to associate the song with my sister. Maybe because her name, like the lead singer of the Pretenders, is Chrissie, with a "y" instead of the singer's "ie." Maybe because it is about sticking together and we—the closest in age of the four children in our family—fought like mad when we were children but also stood by each other, and have been doing so for forty-four years. Even though Chrissy lives in Australia, our regular calls have been part of my morning walks and my quiet evenings in bed.

The song also reminded me of an episode of *Friends* where Chrissie Hynde made a guest appearance, playing at Central Perk with Phoebe. When I lived in the city those kinds of things happened. I missed New York City, but my life there with children already lacked some of the spontaneity of city life in our twenties. We had few responsibilities back then, and no dependents relying on us to make healthcare decisions. One evening after work more than twenty years ago, my sister and I made small talk about skiing with Lou

Reed at his book signing. Around the same time, my friend Moira and I had stopped at a near-empty restaurant in Chelsea between gallery visits one weekend. The only other patron looked up from his book as we talked, and our loud chatter turned to timid smiles when we realized it was Michael Stipe.

Now we made plans carefully and only after calculating risks. Performing arts were mostly canceled, along with the dreams, whimsy, and improvisation they brought to our lives. The Capitol Theatre, our best local connection to live music, had been closed for more than a year. Instead, I listened to my kids' painfully loud trumpet and baritone lessons on Zoom. The little surprises that sparked my imagination came in the form of songs from internet playlists. Standing in the kitchen listening to "I'll Stand by You," I thought, *If someone had asked me a year and a half ago if I'd be more likely to run into Chrissie Hynde in a West Village coffee shop or meet my child at the middle school gym for a mass inoculation, I would have probably bet on Chrissie.* But here we were, in May of 2021. I'd have lost that bet.

And then the tears came, from nowhere and everywhere. I remembered standing next to my son the day before, letting someone stick him with a needle in the hope that it would mean he was kept safe from this invisible threat. Robert's face had been mostly covered by his mask and his long hair, hiding any fear in his dark brown eyes. He used to throw tantrums when he had to get shots. But yesterday, surrounded by classmates, he hadn't even flinched.

One day not long after Rob's vaccination, the archivist at the historical society sent me a text: He'd found the missing record book, spine facing in, on the stacks in the archive. I rushed over to have a look, paging through the book in search of lessons, precedent, hope. I noticed how at first the health officer had written the full word: influenza. After months of fatigue and repetition, he shortened it to flu, and eventually to ditto marks.

All those people were just statistics now, "recovered" or "deceased," names on lines without stories. Who had stood by those people, nursing them to health or carrying on their legacies? Who'd stood by my great-great-grandfather? Where did my children and I fit into our family story, what would we carry with us from my grandmother, who by some miracle had lived for over a century? When June came, her birthday felt more special than ever, not because she had broken the century line and had gone on to add the icing of an additional year, but because we could see her in person for the first time in over a year. We could say, finally, "I'll stand by you," and mean it.

TRACK 14

How You've Grown

"When I grow up, I will eat sweets every day, on the way to work and I will go to bed late every night," Eliza delivered her solo line in our favorite *Matilda* song with a bright clear voice, despite the surgical mask. She stood on a cube with the letter 'Y' on it, the other actors on their own cubes, giant versions of the wooden alphabet blocks we had in our playroom when the kids were toddlers. Eliza wore a blue plaid jumper with a navy blue blazer over it, and repeatedly swept her long shiny brown hair out of her face. She'd worn pigtails earlier in the play, until the evil Ms. Trunchbull tossed her character, Amanda Thripp, by her pigtails. One of Eliza's best friends rode around the stage on a Razor scooter, wearing a matching jumper, long dark brown hair flowing behind her.

About a dozen kids danced, sang, and scooted around the stage for the duration of the three-minute song. It felt magical to watch them again, to remember the last time we were in this auditorium, and to realize how much Eliza had grown up during that long window off stage. In early March 2020, we'd watched Eliza in *Peter Pan* at this same theatre, inside the Jewish Community Center in Scarsdale. My parents, both in their 70s, had attended one of those performances, smiling at their granddaughter from their flip-down seats, unmasked and unprotected. We didn't have masks back then, only a growing sense of dread.

I remembered calling my parents a few days before the play and saying, "The virus is in New Rochelle, Mom. Are you sure you want to come? I mean, what do you think? We'll figure it out if you change your mind." My parents had offered to watch the younger kids while I took Rob to a hockey tournament and Rich went away for work. Life was hectic and once in a while we needed help covering the bases. My parents were still up for it, in hindsight a risky move, and by Sunday, we were all home watching Eliza's play after traveling on planes, staying in hotels, eating in restaurants, and swimming in indoor pools.

A few days later, the National Guard was called in to clean every inch of that same JCC as we shifted our attention from distant China, Italy, and Seattle to our own county. Performances for the following weekend were canceled, and Eliza's acting instructors offered lessons on Zoom to fill the void.

Eliza fell in love with Broadway during kindergarten when I took her to her first show, a matinee of *Matilda*. I picked her and Rob up early from school on one of the last days in June and we took the train into the city. She was five years old, almost six, and wore her hair short, with light brown curls bouncing around her cheeks and chin. One side was fastened back with a barrette, and she wore one of her favorite cotton sundresses. I brought her a sweater in case the theatre was cold. We had moved out of the city only two years earlier, but for the children the memories had receded and the energy and rush of Times Square felt entirely new.

Eliza insisted on holding her own ticket as we waited in line at the Shubert, and once inside, she marveled at the rows of seats and the giant stage. She nearly disappeared in the velvet seat, and the usher gave us a plastic booster so she could see the actors above the shoulders of the person in front of her. Eliza and Robert both watched quietly, mesmerized by the adorable, clear-voiced Matilda, such a contrast to the mean, rough adults trying to ruin her dreams.

When Matilda and her school friends swung on giant swings hung from the top of the theatre, my children gasped and popped up even higher on their bouncy seats. "I wish I had a swing like that," Robert whispered to me. He'd loved swings from the time he was a baby, soothed by the rhythmic motion, and it is no surprise that he finds the kinetic glide of skateboarding up and down ramps similarly reassuring. He still runs to swings at playgrounds, even at twelve years old. Despite my hips feeling a bit squished in the rubber seats, I still love swings, too.

Eliza and her cast did not have fancy swings suspended from the ceiling of the JCC, but they had the nursery blocks and the scooters to give that sense of movement and freedom. Choreography aside, the words in "When I Grow Up" are enough to make any adult's eyes well up with tears. Written as a child's take on what it means to be a grown-up, it focuses on bravery and strength as the attributes that enable us to carry heavy loads, reach high branches, fend off scary creatures, and make our own decisions about sweets and bedtime. Whenever I hear it, I'm reminded that I don't feel particularly brave or strong, only at times unprepared to carry all that weight, and amazed by the depth of love. Longing pulls from both sides—the child eager to grow up, the parents nostalgic for their child's younger years, and perhaps their own.

I'd forgotten to buy Eliza flowers for after the show, but I hugged her and kissed her head and told her how much I loved her. The top of her head now reached my shoulder on a fast upward journey toward my chin, and her face was changing, trading the full cheeks of childhood for the new angles and expressions of adolescence. She scooted off around the parking lot, a stretched-out, long-limbed version of her younger self in *Peter Pan*.

Over the next few days, the *Matilda* song played on rotation with a favorite from my teen years, "How You've Grown" by 10,000 Maniacs. When it was released in 1992, I was on the cusp of feeling grown-up, despite clues around the house indicating otherwise. The family photos, flowered twin bedspread, and pink ten-speed bike hinted at a childhood only recently left behind. In the laundry room closet of my childhood home, we had a set of *Encyclopedia Britannica*, a *Webster's Dictionary*, and a thesaurus. Books held the secrets to mysteries back then, just as they did for Matilda. I looked up the word "chide," wanting to make sure I understood the lyrics clearly: "'Just wait and see.' I remember those words and how they chided me, when patient was the hardest thing to be."

That in-between phase lasts a long time. At seventeen, in my freshman year of college in Ithaca, New York, I'd felt so grown up. My dear childhood friend Drew somehow got tickets for us to see 10,000 Maniacs at a nearby college, and the night before my eighteenth birthday on November 16, 1994, we arrived early to be in the front section of a standing-room-only crowd. After some vigorous screaming and pointing at me, my friends effectively communicated that it was my birthday. The band played while Natalie sang a short and sweet rendition of happy birthday before continuing their set. We then watched the petite Natalie Merchant move from stillness to dancing, from quiet to loud, from joy to sadness as she mined the emotional depths of her latest album. I was wearing a new A-line wool miniskirt over thick tights with Doc Martens, a wardrobe staple I had adopted—along with cowboy boots—while spending twelfth grade in Toronto. I loved my outfit. I loved my life.

After the concert, we waited with a dwindling crowd outside the stage door, hoping to see Natalie in person. Drew used his blue eyes and charismatic smile to try to charm the security guards. "Please, can Natalie come say hello? It's my friend's birthday and it would mean the world to her."

Drew had an unwavering stance, and eventually the guards must have decided a five second hello was preferable to an extended argument with persistent, overconfident college kids. The guard went inside, brought Natalie to the door and cracked it open. Despite being six or seven inches taller, I felt dwarfed by her quiet voice and her calm presence, not to mention her talent. I could feel her annoyance emanating through the narrow opening. I managed to say a quick thank you and look in Natalie's eyes. And with one of those instantaneous shifts in perspective that sometimes happen, I saw the young, impatient, insistent fan that she must have seen. Still, she smiled with kindness and wished me a happy birthday before closing the door. My stomach knotted with the thrill of meeting a star and the embarrassment of pushing too hard.

Eliza was always keenly aware of the mile markers of childhood as she passed them, even when there were no parties, flowers, or balloons. She finished elementary school during the same week as her *Matilda* performance, and kicked off summer by using her allowance to make a big purchase: a mini fridge for cosmetics. She put it on the counter in her bathroom and filled it with face masks, lip glosses and creams she purchased at CVS, and others lifted from my drawers and shelves where they'd lain dormant for years. Perpetually disappointed by my lack of a beauty regimen and apathy towards fashion, she happily shared the products with me, eager to teach me her beauty hacks.

At that age I used to dig through my mom's drawers, taking the Clinique eyeshadows from free gifts, and thinking I knew more than her about fashion, maybe about everything. Someday Eliza will recognize that young girl inside of me, still eager to dress up and sing with my children. No matter how grown up I may be, I'll never be too old to grab the ropes and swing with her.

TRACK 15

Drops of Jupiter

When we were young, we made pyramids in the sand in Ocean City, New Jersey. Our pyramids were not sandcastles sculpted with shovels and water; they were precarious sculptures made up of groups of middle and high school girls. On the first row, three or four girls would arrange themselves, hands and knees in the sand, shoulders and hips aligned with one another. The next row climbed carefully on top, one girl fewer than in the bottom row, knees balanced on two adjacent lower backs, hands between shoulder blades. Once they were steady, the third-row contestants slowly ascended the tower, the lightest one or two girls in the group adjusting each limb until balanced. We lifted our heads and smiled at a parent or sibling holding a 35mm camera, clicking one or two shots before someone screamed in exaggerated pain or tumbled off into the soft sand below.

In the evenings we went to the boardwalk, and when we were

old enough to go by ourselves we abandoned the rides and spent the time strolling past the shops and piers, smiling at boys and spending our allowance on souvenir T-shirts, soft serve ice cream, and funnel cakes. We took pictures at sunset in our best outfits, leaning on the wooden railing with the ocean behind us, the evening sunlight shining on our tanned faces and sun-bleached hair. When the vacation ended and we were back in Pennsylvania, anticipating the start of a new school year, we took the rolls of film to Rite Aid and waited anxiously to see how they turned out. After all these decades, the school years blend together and those few summer weeks, so ephemeral and vital, are crystal clear.

Some of the faces in our sandy pyramids changed over the years, while others, our best friends, remained constant. I had Jessica and Stephanie, my two closest friends from preschool onward. My older sister Chrissy, only one year above us in school, also had two lifelong best friends, Alexa and Laurel. We were part of each other's families, walking in and out of each other's homes unannounced and tagging along on trips to the beach.

When I first took my children to the Ocean City boardwalk in 2014, I pushed Ian in a stroller with the two older kids in tow. Despite tears, tantrums, and messy ice cream cones, it was magical. Walking on that familiar boardwalk felt like being on a movie set of my childhood with the sights, sounds, and smells igniting memories from decades earlier.

"Mom, can I go to Playland?" Ian asked on one completely unscheduled Friday in late July 2021. As a parent of three children who live within walking distance of a boardwalk amusement park, this question was familiar. In pre-pandemic years, when the kids asked this question, Rich and I usually said no and had some good reason for it, and then promised to go "one day this summer." One year the children wised up and discovered that mothers get free admission on Mother's Day, the opening weekend of the season, and voila! We checked Playland off the list and had child-centered Mother's Day plans.

When Ian asked, it had been a long time since I had heard that question and as much as I had avoided it in the past, I missed it now. The previous summer, Rye Playland Amusement Park sat quiet and still, its huge parking lot empty. The only signs of life had been people walking and biking with family, friends, and dogs along the boardwalk at its seaside edge while seagulls, ospreys, and other sea birds flew overhead. Giant pieces of brightly colored metal curved and angled against the sky like a box of crayons flung open and then froze in midair; rides that promised laughter and thrills whenever they might be set in motion again. The doors to Playland Ice Casino, where we usually spent weekends hauling kids to and from hockey, stayed locked all winter.

In the summer of 2021, Playland sprang back to life, and our town seemed to take new pride in it. On Saturday evenings we fell in step with neighbors dragging wagons and chasing after toddlers on scooters, all heading toward the beach to watch the weekly fireworks show. Visitors from all over filled the parks and beaches, and a new restaurant on the pier had delicious food and live music. Our family dinner for Eliza's eleventh birthday ended with Eliza, her friend Maddie, and Ian all standing along the boardwalk, gripping the bars of the fence separating them from Splash Zone, the giant flume ride, hoping the spray would soak their warm, sun-kissed skin. The summer sounds of music, waves, squealing riders, and screeching brakes washed over us.

The week before Ian asked to go to Playland, each of the older children had gone with a friend. It was his turn and he knew it. I quickly texted a neighbor whose daughter Lucy is around the same age and off we went, the three of us, running, skipping, and chattering the whole way. The slow-moving midday ticket line offered a lot of time to plan. Which rides should we go to first? What snacks will we have? Are you scared of the haunted house? Can we have extra money to play games? We measured the kids' heights and slapped on those adhesive bracelets, and after years of saying no, my answer to today's Playland requests was a consistent yes. Yes, you can have Dippin' Dots, even though they remain frozen in their pebble shapes when exposed to hot sunlight in some unholy state of matter; and yes, you can play the games even though they are not included in the price of admission. Lucy and Ian were worthy competitors in the water gun horse racing game, and both rode the mini dragon coaster with their new stuffed animal prizes. The kids grew weary faster than I did in the July heat. Reassured that Playland was here to stay, we walked home sweaty and smiling.

Now, during my quiet morning dog walks, the boardwalk was once again scattered with remnants from the previous day's activities. Mika sniffed along the fence, hoping to inhale a hot dog bun or stray french fry before I tugged her away. A baseball hat rested in a mound of sand, perhaps having come loose from its owner on a ride, and I hung it on the fence in the hope of an unlikely reunion. Even in the empty hours, scents of sugar and deep-fried delicacies mixed with the salty sea air as the maintenance crew swept the paths clean, ready to welcome another day.

The boardwalk, or at least my perception of it, had gone through a transformation similar to when Dorothy landed in Oz. The pre-pandemic version had been in black and white. For years, I had appreciated this collision of history, nature, and tourism, but had moved through it by rote, always rushing to get to the next part of the day, and the details had never come into full focus. Now, with consistent and heightened attention, it became a vivid, full-color, saturated sensory environment. I paused periodically on my walks to take pictures of the scenery, never able to translate the beauty onto the screen of my iPhone.

My newfound, technicolor appreciation for the beach and boardwalk made me choose more carefully which podcasts and music I listened to while I walked. Many mornings, the soundtrack of my walks began with the rhythm of the waves of the Long Island Sound mixed with the theme song of *Desert Island Discs*, "By the Sleepy Lagoon," by Eric Coates. As soon as I heard that dreamy tune and then Lauren Laverne's voice, I knew I was about to be transported to someone else's life while at the same time feeling acutely rooted in my own. In each episode, the guest shared music that was meaningful to them, and recounted the formative memories it evoked. The show balanced inspiration, wanderlust, and therapy, plus tidbits of knowledge that could prove interesting at a cocktail party—if those ever happen again.

One morning in early August, when that episode's guest introduced Bette Midler's song "The Rose," I stopped, sat down on a bench and stared out at the Playland pier and the water below. In my imperfect memory, I associated this song with the movie *Beaches*, a story of lifelong friendship starring Bette Midler and Barbara Hershey. Hershey's character is terminally ill, and she dies at the end. Of course, I knew "Wind Beneath My Wings" was the actual theme song, yet I preferred this one, which brought with it images of Mayim Bialik playing the child version of Bette Midler's character, C.C., intermixed with scenes from my own childhood with Jessica, Stephanie, Alexa, Laurel, and my sister Chrissy.

Jessica and I had been almost exactly the same age as the young C.C. when we saw the film. We used to sing the song C.C. performed on stage, "The Glory of Love," and dance around, part silly, part trying to get the words and tune right: "You've got to give a little, take a little, and let your poor heart break a little." For us as kids, the youthful humor had far outweighed the adult loss and grief.

Thinking about the movie now, thirty years later, it was Hershey's character's death that stood out, and it made me reel. Laurel had died of brain cancer in 2016, leaving Chrissy and Alexa without the third point in their sturdy triangle.

Pausing *Desert Island Discs*, I pulled up a recording of "The Rose" on YouTube, brushing off the realization that this song was not in *Beaches* at all. As I listened, I surveyed our boardwalk, nearly empty at this early hour, its creamy stucco buildings with bright green roofs and Art Deco details reminiscent of the structures that lined my childhood boardwalk in Ocean City, and of Atlantic City (circa 1955), where the two girls had frolicked in the movie. Turning to look south across the water, I saw the rust-colored roofs on the stucco pavilions of Rye Town Park. The Spanish Revival architecture looked like the Ocean City bathhouses where we'd showered and changed when we drove down to the shore for day trips, transitioning with all the other tourists from beach to boardwalk. It had felt a bit embarrassing to use the bathhouses because the teens who were lucky enough to live at the beach all summer called us "shoobies," a slang term from generations earlier for day trippers, mocking people who brought lunches in shoeboxes. When we rented a house there for our family vacations, we would shamelessly call other people "shoobies," snickering at their giant coolers and stuffed beach bags.

Years later, we were far-flung, a global constellation of friendship. Alexa and Jessica stayed in Pennsylvania, still vacationing along the Jersey Shore. Chrissy moved to San Francisco and then Melbourne and Stephanie to Perth: coastal cities with piers and boardwalks on the other side of the world. Anytime I traveled to Los Angeles in my 20's and 30's, I visited Laurel and her family in the endless summer of Venice, California. The Venice boardwalk and Santa Monica pier had some of the sights and smells of New Jersey, with the sticky-sweet salt water taffy swapped out for the sex, drugs, and rock-n-roll of southern California. One Sunday evening, I ate dinner with Laurel and her husband at a Thai restaurant in their neighborhood, waiting until the last minute to call a taxi to the airport and board the red-eye back to a New York winter. As much as I loved home, I never wanted to leave Los Angeles.

"And the soul, afraid of dying, that never learns to live." A part of me ached during the two years Laurel was sick. The pain was tidal. It flowed in when I talked to Chrissy or planned a visit to LA, and receded on other days as I went about my life, shuttling kids and standing on dry land. Sitting on the boardwalk on that August morning with Bette Midler, I could still hear Laurel's laugh carrying on the breeze off the Atlantic Ocean. She could make us laugh about everything, from boobs and tan lines to cold cuts and fried eggs. She definitely would have made fun of me for remembering her with this, the cheesiest of songs. A song that reminded me of Laurel, long before she was sick, was Train's "Drops of Jupiter," particularly this verse:

Can you imagine no love, pride, deep-fried chicken

Your best friend always sticking up for you
Even when I know you're wrong?
Can you imagine no first dance, freeze-dried romance
Five hour phone conversation
The best soy latte that you ever had, and me?

"It's just her," Chrissy said one time when we heard it together on the radio. It was a perfect song for Laurel, with a light, upbeat tune and witty lyrics only partially concealing its depth. I cried often as a kid. Laurel almost never cried, and always stood up for her friends, and we were all a little less afraid because we had her in our lives. Her death drained life of its color for a time. I grieved for Laurel, her family, and for my older sister, who had never known a world without her friend.

The Ferris wheel and roller coasters behind me hung motionless in the morning air, waiting for the gates to open for the day's visitors. It was impossible to measure the amount of laughter and joy one single car on a rollercoaster had generated over the years, or calculate the number of dreams awakened at the peak of the Ferris wheel, a shimmering sea stretched out below. A hundred years of postcards and photographs of beaches, boardwalks, and amusement parks could not capture the magic of being there and living life in full color with people we love. From then on, the answer would be yes.

TRACK 16

Radio Ga Ga

"Should I enter the competition? I don't think so. Well, maybe. Yeah, I think I can do it." Rob cycled through these thoughts a few times at various moments in the days leading up to our trip to Montauk. On a Friday in late August, we'd learned through a friend about a skateboarding competition and fundraiser to launch a renovation of the Montauk Skatepark. Registration was around lunchtime on Sunday, and with very little information beyond that, he and I packed his boards and drove.

Rob had started skateboarding a few years earlier, and we had made occasional trips to this park. It is old-school, carved out of a cement parking lot with a giant bowl in the shape of a kidney-bean swimming pool. The bowl has a shallow end and a deep end, and every time I see my kids venture down into the depths I realize if I had to go in there, it would be physically impossible for me to get myself out again without a ladder and a rescue team. As a kid, it had been exhilarating to run up and down the halfpipes my older brother Sam and his friends had built—all that speed and freedom. My friend Jessica and I watched these high school boys with awe. They were too old and too removed from our fifth-grade lives to be our crushes. They were closer to celebrities, or heroes. When they took snack breaks, Jessica and I ran up and down the ramps, just as my younger kids do now on the collection of mini ramps we have in our driveway, a covid engineering project. Our neighbors on the other side of the fence generously and patiently refer to my son as Tony Hawk. I assure them that Tony knows the skate park does not open until eight a.m.

That rhythmic whirring of wheels on concrete, multiplied by thirty, filled the hot summer air on that afternoon in Montauk. As soon as we arrived Rob rode off, his baggy jeans and oversized black T-shirt disappearing in the crowd of skaters. He quickly made friends as they warmed up on the elements, and soon their hellos turned to laughter and cheers. I chatted with our new acquaintances who'd invited us, and with a skateboard instructor, Russ, whom I recognized from the previous summer by his signature dreadlocks and encouraging manner.

The skate culture was thick in the air, with parents talking about skate parks in and around New York City and kids helping each other with tricks and filming. A few merchandise tents selling beanies, T-shirts, and decks lined the flat asphalt area adjacent to the skate park. The sun radiated off the concrete, and I could feel my bare shoulders getting burned through the sunscreen. A group of girls hung back along the chain-link fence, their perfectly applied makeup so thick I wondered how it stayed in place on this hot, cloudless day. Their black eyeliner matched the black in their plaid skirts and leather belts, while white button-down shirts tied at the waist created a stark contrast to their bright red lipstick. They reminded me of the goth kids in my high school, but I know Rob and Eliza would correct me and tell me the appropriate word is emo. Whatever song was playing at that moment, my mind jumped to Tom Petty's "Free Fallin'":

All the vampires, walking through the valley,
Move west down Ventura Boulevard,
And all the bad boys are standing in the shadows,
And the good girls are home with broken hearts.

The scene surrounding me could have been somewhere in LA or the Valley, where I imagined it would be easy to find skaters clustered on any given day. But here in Montauk in a normally empty skate park, it felt like a once in a lifetime experience.

I took a few photos and videos of Rob and the other skaters as they moved through the park, their agile figures gliding against a background of brightly-graffitied concrete lines and shapes. I love graffiti; it's a feature of my New York City life that I had never considered I might miss when I weighed the options and moved to the suburbs. Pulsing music blared from the registration booth. The scene was like a well-choreographed dance on a vibrant stage, the skaters constantly swiveling out of one another's way, changing direction, speed, height, and angle so that no two seconds had the same composition. The music pulsed along with them, a playlist from my generation and Rob's generation mixed together, and I found myself singing out loud, my voice drowned out by all the other noise.

Opening the Notes app on my phone, I decided to preserve the moment and ran back through the half dozen songs we had already heard and started to list them. Queen's "Radio Ga Ga" was playing as I typed, and at the line, "You made us feel like we could fly," I looked up to see these children and teenagers flying to the music. Kids passed their phones back and forth to take video clips for one another, just as Sam and his friends had filmed each other using our giant RCA camcorder back in the '80s. He had a drawer full of VHS tapes, some from their skate sessions, and some copies of skate movies like *Thrashin'*. When Sam went to college in 1988, I used to go into his room—the garage my parents converted much like Greg Brady's groovy bedroom—and flip through his mix tapes and VHS collection. Skateboarding has the same appeal for these kids as it did for my brother and his friends in the '80s: transportation, sport, creativity, art, freedom, music, friendship.

I called out to Rob, now shirtless and hanging out with a bunch of other kids on the top of a ramp, half with shirts, half without, to offer him some water. *At least they all had helmets on*, I thought. I asked if he wanted to sign up for the competition. "Yes!" he replied, no longer hesitant. He wrote his name on the list of 13-17-year-olds, having celebrated his thirteenth birthday a few weeks earlier. The man running the competition explained the format, saying, "It's all good, it's all friendly. We just want the kids to have fun out there and see some awesome skating." Rob rolled off and the competition soon began.

As the songs played, I remembered a recent interview I'd heard with Martha Quinn to commemorate the 40th Anniversary of MTV. I still picture her twenty-something face on our box-shaped television, the focal point of our split-level suburban home with wall-to-wall carpeting and wood-paneled walls. While any respectable MTV fan knew that the first song played on the network was "Video Killed the Radio Star," "Radio Ga Ga" had been one of my favorite early videos. "Radio" had given Freddie Mercury's generation of teenagers a window to the outside world; the black and white music video shows radio as a source of color and light. MTV introduced a new medium for music, combining two art forms to tell stories. The technology changes, and the specific artists and songs change, but not the need for music.

Listening to the playlist at the skatepark, many of the songs hadn't actually changed. The Beastie Boys, New Order, and Talking Heads—which I'd first heard on my brother's boombox—were still here, mixed in with Pearl Jam, Outkast, and Green Day, covering the decades between then and now. "Cupid's Chokehold" by Gym Class Heroes spanned two generations and two genres at the same time, a hip-hop song with a chorus featuring Supertramp's 1979 hit "Breakfast in America." This was a new one for me, but of course my kids learn some "old" music through samples, and I wasn't surprised that Rob knew this song.

Other than the newest songs, I had seen most of the DJ's picks as music videos in my teen years. MTV introduced a new term to the world, VJ, and Martha Quinn was my favorite VJ on the network. If she were at this event, I was sure there would have been more female singers featured—The Pretenders, Blondie, Suzanne Vega. Even back then I had a sense that Martha was good at her job, loved what she was doing, and was creating a new category for what was possible. She was only half a generation older, and she taught us that a woman could do something in the world not because of how she looked but because she had something to say.

As I watched these skaters, many of whom were probably also artists, musicians or otherwise talented and passionate kids, it reminded me how important it is to believe in young people. I remembered the rough outline of Martha's story, that she'd been a senior at NYU working part-time as the person who restocks toilet paper in the dorms, and happened to hear about the auditions for this new network. Someone suggested she should go, and she rode off in a cab. It helps to be in the right place at the right time, and when there's an opportunity, to follow its path. On that bright, hot, loud day with the skater community in Montauk, Rob was right where he belonged. He didn't win the contest, but he got a taste of what it feels like to fly.

TRACK 17

Zombie

Summer turned to fall, and it seemed we had turned a corner for good this time, with school starting again in September 2021 and the "new normal" everyone discussed beaming like the light at the end of the tunnel. We hadn't reached the light, but it was bright enough and close enough to lead us out. School days started around eight a.m. and ended at three p.m., no one was home at lunchtime, and the Google Classroom interface faded from my visual memory.

Then we got the call. My son Ian, too young to be vaccinated, had had close exposure to someone who tested positive. Quarantine. Watch for symptoms. For real this time. We tested the whole family, and we were all negative. We then shut Ian in his bedroom, an eight-year-old left to his own devices, quite literally. He watched something called *Annoying Orange*, and a lot of rock videos. Ian's very close friend is a rock aficionado, and they'd been set to start guitar lessons together the following week. Now it would be the following following week, or whatever that's called, after we emerged from the ten-day dark hole.

When Ian tested positive on day two of his quarantine, we weren't surprised. He was healthy, barely a sniffle, but he coughed twice and off we went for a rapid test. More bowls of cereal delivered to his door, egg sandwiches on a good morning, plates left outside in the hallway, and a new box of N95 masks for all of us to wear inside our home. "Grimmy grimsters," Rich commented. There wasn't a much more eloquent way to describe this new reality. The reassuring thing, of course, was that our child was basically fine. Ian's symptoms cleared faster than a regular cold, he never had a fever, and he learned to bathe himself in the bathroom that only he was allowed to enter. Check that life lesson off my to-do list.

But those days dragged on as we waited to see if we'd have breakthrough cases and if Eliza, also too young for the vaccine, would get sick. Every little thing—a tension headache, a throat-clearing cough in the morning—caused me to catastrophize, my anxiety visceral as I imagined various worst-case-scenarios. And so I walked, masked and bundled, hidden and distanced from familiar unmasked faces I passed along the boardwalk where I'd carved a path back in spring of 2020.

I'd had it with podcasts about covid and vaccines. We were done with that, right? So I listened to *The Moth Radio Hour*, *Selected Shorts*, and *Desert Island Discs*. We had groceries delivered again, but cooked without any of the enthusiasm of the previous year. No "Look! I made a pie!" pictures would grace my Facebook feed. The picture now would be, "Look! I put a bowl of Special K outside my kid's bedroom door!" We gave Ian some time alone in the yard each day, which he spent throwing knives into an upright piece of plywood. His best friend is also into martial arts and had given him some Japanese knives called *kunai*. Throwing knives seemed perhaps the perfect way to pass the time during covid recess.

It felt like forever, but after about five days, Ian's tests were negative, and calm settled in once again. Still no school for a few more days, but at least I had bright, warm fall days trapped together with the people I loved. The kids, still separated and masked indoors, started spending as much time as possible outside playing soccer. Ian had never liked town soccer, where he didn't quite understand the rules, but with his dad and sister, he was in heaven. And not half bad at it either.

With everyone playing outside, I declared it time for a pandemic house cleaning reminiscent of the previous year. "I'm playing my screaming women music!" I warned from the sliding door to the backyard. Ian cried out in response, "It's in your heeeaaaad, in your heyaahead. Zombie. Zombie. Zombeheheheh." I let out a proud laugh. So Ian had been listening all along. Then he told me that his best friend, the eight-year-old rocker, loved that song, as if to say, "No, Mom, don't get an ego. I don't listen to what YOU like." While folding laundry in my bedroom, I caught flashes of Ian out the window, decorating our front yard for Halloween. The haphazard display of flimsy foam graves, a couple of threadbare zombies, skeleton bones, a coffin, and a bloody head with a rat in its mouth felt heavier this year and more ridiculous at the same time.

That afternoon, the sun seemed brighter when I went out for my walk. Checking my podcast subscriptions, the choice was obvious: Tracey Ullman had recently been interviewed on *Desert Island Discs*, and it was right there at the top of the list. I pushed play and stepped back in time to my childhood bedroom, where at eleven or twelve my parents had decided I was old enough to have my own television with the basic channels. Sunday nights in middle school were my version of Ian's parent-free quarantine. I curled up alone in my room, under the flowered bedspread of my four-post twin bed, and watched my favorite lineup, *The Tracey Ullman Show* and *Married... with Children*. Like the rest of America, this was how I met *The Simpsons*. Hearing her voice reminiscing about her comedic skits and wacky characters, I remembered being that young person, about the same age as Robert and Eliza now, laughing out loud in my bedroom at Tracey's British accent and her many characters. She'd brought comedy to life for me back then, and as I listened to this podcast, a lightness returned with each step I took along the sturdy boards.

Humor is a binding force, and a necessary ingredient for getting through these long months. Our family's favorite *Saturday Night Live* sketches during lockdown had become a part of our dialect, and after we'd exhausted the ones filmed over Zoom, we launched into a study of characters from SNL seasons past. My kids could recite "Dad Prank Video" with Mikey Day and his son ("It's your boy, Brandon!") from memory, and they threatened to change all my phone contacts to Gigi Hadid in honor of the sketch. We'd watched *The Wonder Years* reboot the previous March, and afterward Rob introduced us to the skit, "Hip Hop Classics: Before They Were Stars." In the skit, Flavor Flav gives the voiceover for Kevin in the signature scene of *The Wonder Years* where he gives Winnie Cooper his jacket. We watched Chris Farley as Matt Foley the motivational speaker, and Pete Davidson as Chad countless times, and my kids learned that behind all their beloved SNL characters were real people with real problems.

As I listened to Tracey Ullman now, I got to know the person beneath the jokes—her dedication to acting, her love for her family. One of the *Desert Island* songs she chose was an old favorite of mine by Elvis Costello that I hadn't listened to in years. I had always interpreted it as a lighthearted love song, but listening now, I heard it as more of a life lesson: that each day I have choices as my story unfolds, "Everyday, everyday, everday I write the book."

Live music had finally started up again, not long before Ian tested positive. When our quarantine officially ended and our children were back in school again, I checked the lineup at The Capitol Theatre—Brian Wilson that week, Elvis Costello the next month. Rich and I bought last-minute tickets to see Brian Wilson and a couple other Beach Boys, finally crossing the threshold into the historic theatre again after being away so long. We were too nervous to sit in our assigned seats and hung at the back, in what used to be the Standing Room Only section, back when big crowds were still allowed.

The theatre filled our senses with nostalgia as we stood, feet rooted on worn carpets, leaning on wood railings, looking up at the carved balcony boxes and ornate ceiling as the brilliant acoustics carried the music. I sent my parents video clips of some of their favorite songs, music they sang along to in the car while my siblings and I rolled our eyes and covered our ears with Walkman headphones. We had now become those parents, and after years of singing it to our children on car rides, Rich got to hear "Sloop John B" live.

A few weeks later, I rounded up a few neighbors to see Elvis Costello. We now felt safe sitting on the flip-down velvet theatre seats, a welcome upgrade offering a much better view of the show. Elvis Costello was lively and clever, filling the spaces between songs with little jokes or stories to give context. His keyboard player was unable to make it at the last minute, leaving a hole onstage and a reminder that all plans are subject to change these days. Still, the show went on. He didn't sing "Everyday I Write the Book," but he sang many of his other hits, including, at the very end, "Alison." Along with all the other Alisons, Allisons, and Allysons born in the mid-1970s, I was sure he was singing it just for me.

The following week, when my kids went trick-or-treating, Ian was dressed in a full-body black Morphsuit—a body stocking of sorts that included a head covering. He looked like a ninja, or maybe a metaphor for a virus, but for some reason the song "Zombie" played again in my head. As a teenager, I had seen the video on MTV and worked to learn the lyrics, gaining some superficial knowledge of the Troubles in Ireland through words and footage. That Halloween, though, I put the true meaning of the song aside as I watched children and adults of all ages running around, eating pizza and candy with friends on streets that had been nearly empty the year before. Dressed as heroes, characters, dreams, death, terror, and comedy, we trampled suburban yards strewn with spooky decorations, a bunch of zombies finally emerging from our houses, alive again.

TRACK 18

All for Love

We got to see our families for Thanksgiving in year two of covid. That was something, right? Better than the year before. Had we taken tests before we saw them? Gosh, who could remember, though we could have gotten tests anywhere—any CVS or Rite Aid—back in November! But December? December was epic, particularly in the New York City area with the giant wave of Omicron and the continued ripples of Delta surrounding us on all sides. We whittled down our plans with family to a Christmas Day outdoor drive-by with my parents and tested before the holiday, but despite our efforts, Rob and I spent the last few days of December isolating in a hotel room in Georgia, both of us positive for covid.

When Ian had tested positive in September, it had been a bit stressful, and felt like life stopped still and changed course. This time it was far less jarring, even though Rob was the child I had worried about the most, with his history of asthma and pneumonia.

Luckily, he had almost no symptoms and mine were mild. We were fine, just somewhat radioactive and very bored.

The Impractical Jokers were still on television around the clock, just as they had been when we were in Georgia in April. We had books and other resources to keep us busy, but left the show on for background noise if we were doing something else. Mostly though, we did nothing else. Rob and I couldn't get enough of these four high school friends from Staten Island embarrassing one another.

When I hit an all-time low and realized I was watching an episode I had seen just the day before, I scrolled through the channels to find something else. Rob was already asleep at eight-thirty, knocked out by pure boredom or by the melatonin we had both been taking at a friend's suggestion. I landed on *Say Anything*, Cameron Crowe's 1989 movie, just before Diane Court breaks up with Lloyd Dobler. The day before I had watched the last half hour of *Almost Famous*. For a minute I felt guilty that I might be missing a Cameron Crowe marathon for *Impractical Jokers*. Of course I also have Netflix on my laptop. I could have been watching pretty much anything.

At one point during isolation, I tried to hook Rob on *Arrested Development*, but three episodes in I fell asleep and he went back to *Impractical Jokers*. Watching one movie together from beginning to end seemed like an attainable quarantine goal, and as the credits rolled to the music of Nancy Wilson's "All for Love," I decided that movie would be *Say Anything*. Rob loves skateboarding and '80s culture, so how could he not connect with the kickboxing-crazed, music-loving Lloyd Dobler? I told him the plan right after breakfast the next morning. With the expected thirteen-year-old reluctance, he settled in by the time Lloyd and Diane graduated Lakewood High.

Rob was exactly the same age I was when I first saw *Say Anything* in the theatre, just barely qualifying for entry to the PG-13 film. He didn't want to admit he liked the movie, but he liked the movie. Lloyd is undeniably likable, as are most of the characters. There's no bad guy in this movie, no bully, at least on the teen level. I suddenly realized what makes these Cameron Crowe movies different from some other coming-of-age movies, something I'd never paid attention to when I was younger: the parents are complex, and they create the tension and the obstacles more than any peer dynamics do. When I was a teenager, I'd been so focused on Lloyd and Diane, on Will and Penny Lane, that I didn't pay much attention to Diane's corrupt dad, Lloyd's absent parents, or Will's controlling mom. Their role was to create a problem to drive the plot, nothing more.

Watching as an adult, I saw Diane's father and Lloyd's older sister—a single mom—very differently. They are having their own crises, going through their own growing pains, making sometimes irreversible mistakes, full of regret. While I'd been blind to this as a teen, the younger characters in the movies recognize their parents' flaws, or come to discover them in heartbreaking ways. Maybe that is what makes a movie timeless. We watch it from one perspective the first time, and then we encounter it later on a different level.

Rob and I both laughed at Lloyd's nervous talking and at his little nephew, but Rob might not have felt the pain I did when Lloyd left his older sister and nephew alone at the end to go to London with Diane. Rob definitely noticed that Diane's dad is very controlling, and maybe it helped him appreciate that, at least with his skateboarding and music, we do give him some freedom to be himself.

Some things never change. Others do: Rob laughed out loud at the boombox scene. I don't know what inspired his laughter more— the concept of a boombox as a source of music, or being so in love with a girl that you would stand outside her house in a trench coat holding a boombox playing "In Your Eyes." I had memorized all the words to Peter Gabriel's whole album; "In Your Eyes" was our prom song one year. Watching the movie now for the millionth time, the Nancy Wilson song caught my attention. It was the lyric "And make music out of madness" that surprised me. Making music out of madness was a great way to describe what we had been doing for over a year and a half. Googling the song, I learned that Nancy Wilson wrote all the songs that Corey, Lloyd's best friend, sings about her ex-boyfriend, Joe. Long before Adele's latest album and Olivia Rodrigo's litany of break-up songs, there was Corey, who wrote sixty-three songs, all of them about Joe.

As the movie ended, I tucked it into my mental pocket of things we might never have done if not for the pandemic. Rob tested negative later that day and could re-enter the world, a little tiny version of a happy ending.

The next morning, I woke before dawn on New Year's Day and watched *CODA*, alone now in my isolation room. When I finished, I resolved to watch it again with my children someday, hopefully soon, when we were together again. During my morning walks listening to *Desert Island Discs*, the song that I heard most frequently selected on people's lifetime soundtracks was Joni Mitchell's "Both Sides Now." As many times as I'd heard that song, I had never listened to it the way I did when it played in *CODA*. The movie's writer and director, Sian Heder, explores family love and the burdens and gifts we give our children, all heightened by an exceptionally realistic portrayal of adolescence and belonging. Ruby and her friend Miles have real problems, big problems, much like Lloyd and Diane. I shifted back to the teen perspective, perhaps because it was my first viewing, and made a mental note to listen a bit more to my children.

As the new year began, I thought about how I'd looked at life from many sides by now, in ways I'd never imagined—from a child's eyes, a mother's eyes, and the eyes of my aging family members. I'd seen it from both sides of quarantine, injury, illness, joy, fear, optimism, hopelessness, and from the inside and outside of my home. Those months and years were far from perfect, but at some point we had let go of striving for any ideal. It was a time full of laughter and tears and dreams never realized for both children and adults, and other dreams born in the empty spaces left behind.

No matter how many times I reminded my children that we had to be flexible and take things one day at a time, it was hard not to feel lost in the uncertainty. Sometimes I went for a walk or listened to music alone in my room to escape because I felt so much pressure to fix the pain, to take care of their needs, to make everyone's life okay. Then I'd see Eliza choreographing a new dance, or Rob transcribing the lyrics to his favorite hip-hop songs, or Ian practicing a chord from Green Day on his new guitar. We made music out of madness; maybe that is what life is about. Or maybe, as Joni Mitchell sings, "It's life's illusions I recall. I really don't know life at all."

TRACK 19

Good Riddance

I f my kids ever ask me to go camping, I'll remind them that we did that one night in Ladysmith, Virginia, stuck between two exits and thousands of vehicles on I-95 North. Then they will never ask again.

Shouldn't getting covid on vacation have been enough? When we told the school Rob and I tested positive, they advised us to keep our kids remote for the beginning of the next week. So we extended our time away from home by a day, just to be safe, before all piling into the car together and driving north. We planned to stay overnight near Richmond, and when we hit that area around eight p.m., traffic was moving well. We stopped for a quick dinner and got back on the highway, hoping to cover just a bit more distance before finding a hotel for the night. North of Richmond, south of Fredericksburg, the interstate was suddenly slick and icy and I pulled out my iPhone to start looking for nearby hotels.

"When my brother lived in Charlottesville, he always said Virginia can't handle snow," I mentioned as we cruised past Exit 104. We decided to get off at the next exit, Exit 110 according to Google Maps. In a few miles, we slowed to a crawl with all the lanes filled. We moved to the slightly faster-moving left lane to avoid being behind a truck, and settled in behind a blue sedan, noting that a couple vehicles had slid off the highway into the median. Others had tried to turn around and head south, getting stuck in the process. As we rolled to a stop, we never imagined we would remain behind that blue sedan for the next fourteen hours. The temperature dropped to the low twenties and the trucks and cars around us froze to a standstill, engines running, tail lights illuminating a never-ending stretch of highway. We called hotels near that elusive Exit 110 and as the kids nodded off to sleep, Rich and I said all kinds of things that sounded so naive in retrospect.

"I bet it is an accident and once they get it moved, we'll get going."

"Google Maps didn't show the traffic until much further north, around DC."

"Now Google Maps says it will take two hours to get to Fredericksburg! That's insane."

"Kids, go to sleep, we'll get you up when we get to a hotel and you can do remote school there in the morning."

Around eleven p.m., a father and son from the minivan behind us came to our window, a billowing cloud of breath meeting the cold air as they asked to use our phone. They said we were going to be there a long time—they'd heard the whole highway was closed. I gave an incredulous look. "Should we just go to sleep?" I asked. "That's what we are doing," the son answered.

Our kids slept, and Rich sort of slept, but I stared at the red tail lights. Any time I dozed off, I woke up again to the sound of the truck next to us turning on its engine. Like us, it seemed to be rotating on a schedule, turning on for heat and then off again to conserve gas. Thankfully, we had nearly a full tank, having filled up on our last stop.

Someone came by and asked for jumper cables, and while we couldn't help him with that, I loaned him my phone to call his cousin in Lansdale. "Lansdale! I'm from Malvern, near Valley Forge!" I mentioned, excited to talk to someone outside of our car. He was parked up near the yellow Penske truck I'd been staring at for hours, about four vehicles ahead in the left lane.

Sometime after midnight, Rich and I discussed the best way to heat the car. I kept turning off the engine when he dozed off, hesitant to keep it running in case we twitched and hit the center console, knocking the car into gear. While the worry seemed illogical, I knew I couldn't handle a fender bender in this situation. Rich, on the other hand, wanted to stay warm. In the end he slept while I adjusted the ignition, the temperature, and my emotions as necessary.

Rob woke up around three a.m. to go to the bathroom and asked where we were. When we broke the news that we had not moved, his anxiety and discomfort with both the larger situation and his sleeping position led to a panic that woke the other two children. Now we were helping all three children make their first trip to the "bathroom," a makeshift stall we formed by opening both doors on one side of the car. With the cargo of a tractor trailer on one side and a snowy shoulder on the other, we had adequate privacy for an emergency situation. After they finished, we dug out coats from suitcases in the back and rearranged the children with Rob in the third row and Eliza and Ian lying head-to-toe across the middle seat. At the very moment I made a silent wish that no one kicked the other in the face, someone kicked someone in the face. Adjustments, arguments, some push-and-pull, and then quiet. Sometime between four and five, I gave up on sleep and started to read instead, a close bond forming between me and the post-pandemic caravan in Emily St. John Mandel's *Station Eleven*.

The worrisome, sleepless night on the highway ended in the reassuring way that any stressful night ends, with the sky brightening before the sunrise ushers in a new day. With everyone else still sleeping, I started to come to terms with the new reality of our situation and fired off a few brief emails to my children's teachers, letting them know not to expect Ian and Eliza on Google Meet. *Unless things improve quickly*, I added, a last sliver of optimism.

While we had not seen any police cars or other official vehicles since we'd rolled to a stop, I had a growing understanding of the severity of this traffic jam thanks to neighboring vehicles and a couple desperate phone calls. Texting with a few early bird friends back home as they started their morning routines, the picture crystalized. This was, in fact, a shitshow of epic proportions, and was the main news story on *Good Morning America* and the *Today* show. Even Senator Tim Kaine was stuck! Links to story after story of what went wrong and how people helped one another filled my text inbox. I put my book down, enjoying this very personal version of doom scrolling. It even had a name: *Nightmare on 95*. At least I had something to share with the kids when they woke up and realized we were still stuck behind that blue sedan.

No one in our car could sleep through anyone else's bathroom trip. A visit to the bathroom, no matter how brief, meant that the temperature inside the car dropped about twenty degrees in under a minute, and then Rich turned the heat back on at full blast, prompting comments a few minutes later that it was getting stuffy. The remote school lesson for the day was a chemistry experiment on states of matter as the kids competed over who could melt the most ice on a bathroom break. Soon after sunrise, everyone had returned to vertical positions and we turned the music on again as I shared news highlights.

We'd had a running rotation of music on that road trip. Each of us took a turn selecting a song to play on Spotify, and the only rule was that no one could request the same song twice in one day. The rule's simplicity did not make it easier to follow; the children would beg to hear their favorite "just one more time." We held strong, no song more than once a day—until Snowmaggedon. Ian's first request was Green Day's "Good Riddance," a song that marked such formative moments as the final episode of *Seinfeld* and my college graduation—and now this, a situation in which the lyrics, "Another turning point, a fork stuck in the road," could be applied more literally.

It was hard not to laugh at the absurdity, the number of factors that had to align in order for us to end up here, on this highway, for the past ten hours. Then Rob chose Chief Keef's "Laughin' to the Bank," and just like that, we laughed.

Some of us cried, too. At least two of us, but I will not reveal names. There were yelps of hunger when the half bag of rest stop popcorn was gone. Some tense backseat negotiations over a dwindling supply of candy and gum forced me out of the car, closing the door tight behind me. I wandered coatless between the parked vehicles, shuffling on the ice and savoring the fresh air and relative quiet. A truck driver next door was stretching his legs, too.

"Do you need anything? Water?" he asked. *Need* was an interesting word and it took me a few seconds to answer. The kids were not dehydrated, but yes, they were thirsty.

"I have three kids in the car. A water would be great." He emerged with three waters and three mandarin oranges, and I returned to our car a hero after my sanity break. We had missed our chance to tell our story to *The New York Times* or *Good Morning America* as some other unlucky families did from the cold depths of the night, and we still had no idea how long we would be stuck as we approached the twelve-hour mark. Rich grabbed a football from the back of the car and the kids piled out to toss the ball and explore the highway. The fresh air, still well below freezing, felt much warmer in the bright sun. I posted something on Instagram. More texts. More stories. This news story had made it to the west coast, and even to a friend in New Zealand. "Did you meet Senator Tim Kaine?" she asked.

Somehow, everyone stuck on the highway survived the nightmare. People were freezing cold, some with babies, toddlers, elderly relatives, and pets in tow. Some missed scheduled surgeries; one family missed a funeral. But no one froze to death or got hypothermia. Truck drivers were the heroes, offering warmth and water along the forty-five mile stretch of stillness. In a generous and biblical gesture, a bread truck on a different section of highway opened its cargo, and people walked around distributing loaves to all the nearby cars. It reminded me of a meme I saw early in the pandemic, my old friend Mr. Rogers with a caption that said, "When I was a boy and I would see scary things in the news, my mother would say to me, 'Look for the helpers. You will always find people who are helping.'"

Leaving a large group of tired, cold, and frustrated people to fend for themselves seems like a recipe for disaster; it was a relief that kindness ruled the day. With no one there to blame, and surrounded by others trapped in varying degrees of the same misfortune, the collective attitude was one of patience and calm. We did not see a single person of authority until around eleven a.m., and then it was a lone state trooper on foot carrying none of the fuel and water that CNN.com had said was coming our way. The helpers were truck drivers and regular people, offering any assistance they could. In the late morning sun, cars began inching along the two-mile journey to the exit, weaving between the parked eighteen-wheelers and waving each other forward. One good Samaritan in a small red sedan got out to chip and shovel the ice in the right lane and shoulder every time he stopped, making it just a little bit safer for drivers to navigate. It took two hours to move two miles. Inside our vehicle, despite moments of tension, we knew, eventually, we would get home.

Google Maps kept directing us back to I-95, but there was no way we would follow that advice, even if it proved to be faster. I had my first coffee of the day around two p.m., knowing that I would have to power through until we made it home to New York. My kids ate pretzels and Twix from a grocery store because the line at the nearest McDonald's was so long it wrapped around the parking lot and out to the road. Stocked up with gas, coffee, and junk food, we took videos on winding roads of the trees weighed down by snow, a wonderland of shimmering woods stretched out on either side of the narrow driving lane. Avoiding the Washington DC area, we drove a scenic route along Route 301 from Virginia into Maryland, crossing the Chesapeake Bay Bridge from Annapolis to the Eastern Shore. The seaside villages lit up in the snow could have been Christmas cards or Norman Rockwell paintings for the cover of *The Saturday*

Evening Post. No one else in my family appreciated the views from our windows, but I did. By the time we journeyed up the on-ramp of I-95 near Wilmington, Virginia, a wave of relief mixed with my exhaustion. Rich and I took turns driving and sleeping for the rest of the drive, and around eleven p.m., we were finally home.

It used to feel like a small failure to miss a flight or have bad weather on a much-anticipated vacation. Not anymore. Illness, isolation, and a night on a frigid, icy highway became worthy material for memories as the lingering pandemic washed away all notions of a perfect holiday. It was very unpredictable, and nothing felt quite right. Still, we sort of had the time of our lives.

TRACK 20

I'll Be Your Mirror

"It looks like she's doing laundry, so I think it should go in the laundry room," Eliza argued when I showed her my new framed photograph. I was searching for a spot in the dining room to hang the artwork, an image of a woman standing in a doorway holding a wash basin, her hair wrapped loosely in a towel and her body draped in a thin floral robe. The woman's figure was framed in a glowing light, a modern composition with a nod to Vermeer. She gazed downward and to the side. The viewer could not meet her gaze, and the light and shadows drew the eye to the delicate lines of her silhouette instead. After initially feeling this artwork may be too intimate for the dining room, Rich supported my choice, noting how the colors complemented the neutral tones in the wallpaper and the frame was the perfect size, positioned between two large windows. Coordination won him over, and just like that, we had an unfamiliar woman in our dining room, permanently carrying a wash basin.

While Eliza theorized that the woman was doing laundry, to me it looked like she'd just finished bathing and had dumped the warm water out of the basin after blanketing her damp body in a robe. Perhaps it was warm where she lived, and private, and she bathed outdoors or by an open window, the photographer snapping the photo as she carried the basin to its usual spot on the clay tile floor in her bathroom. I pictured her hanging the towel and the damp washcloth over the rim of the basin to dry. I chose this piece of art as a gift to myself during the pandemic because I was drawn to this woman's story, or rather, I liked imagining her story. The only fact I knew about her was her name, Ane. I knew that because the piece was called "Ane."

Finding the work had been a mini saga. I was listening to music and writing very late one night, or early one morning, in the spring. I paused to watch some videos on YouTube and read up on some musicians. At one point, I pulled up the lyrics to The Velvet Underground song "I'll Be Your Mirror" and maybe I clicked on the images tab. It was one of those rabbit hole moments and I do not know exactly how I arrived at an artist's series of photos by the same title, but there I was, tabbing through portraits of people in bathroom mirrors. A friend of ours had read the lyrics to "I'll Be Your Mirror" in our 2007 wedding ceremony, and while I had not been looking for a souvenir from these months locked in our house, an image of a woman in her home felt right.

The artist and I exchanged emails, and in the fall I met him in his Brooklyn studio to see the print and transport it safely home in its cardboard packaging. I learned a little more about Ane, a Venezuelan musician and folk singer, and played her music one day in my kitchen. Still moving through the world as if stuck in molasses, it took me some time to bring it to the framer where it stayed through the hectic holiday season and into the quiet of January.

With three shots and Omicron antibodies coursing through my veins, in mid-January I went on an overnight trip to visit my grandmother, now 101 ½ years old. Once a person passes the centennial it makes sense to count half years again, like a preschooler. We had tea and I showed her pictures of my kids. We ventured to CVS for a birthday card for my niece and a few sympathy cards. "I keep a few of these handy because people are always dying," she explained.

We had lunch and talked, and I poked around in cabinets and shelves at her request that I take anything I'd like. My grandmother, with the right marketing, could challenge Marie Kondo with her decluttering skills. Her sparsely-furnished apartment has a fraction of the keepsakes and photos from the larger Pennsylvania home she shared with my grandfather for decades. Here, every item is familiar and has its own spot.

When I drove home the next day I carried a piece of Stangl pottery, a glass tray, and a bag full of books in the trunk of my car. My grandmother has read so many books. They are the only thing that piles up in her home. Turning off the highway and into my town, I remembered "Ane" at the framer and finally picked her up too, somewhat hesitant to bring more stuff into my overstuffed home.

When "Ane" arrived, the house was a mess from the holidays, the winter weather, the hands, the feet, the food, and the dog. Our walls were marked with smudges, smears, nicks, and chipped paint from all this time at home. The hundred-year-old wooden floors were scratched beyond repair by the dog, the rollerblades, the skateboards, and all the families that came before us. Bookshelves overflowed, messy configurations of hardcovers, paperbacks, writer's notebooks and photo albums. From small to large, children's literature to literary fiction, poetry to prose, and on the bottom shelf, a few well-intended parenting books that will never see the light of day—the books glared at me.

The photo was easy to place on the dining room wall with Rich's help and Eliza's constructive feedback. I tucked away the pottery and tray for use with future guests. The bag of hand-me-down books, complete with Post–it notes written to my grandmother from her friends and neighbors, needed spots. In a process of purging and organizing and carrying games, books, and albums up and down stairs, I made space for the new books and considered what to keep and what to give away. I picked up the tiniest of books, a treasured thank-you gift from my friend Margot.

Maira Kalman's limited edition *Women Holding Things* is a work of art and a keepsake. With concise words and powerful, uncomplicated images she tells the story—poetic and lyrical—of women. When Margot gave me this gift last spring, I'd been holding too many other things to fully appreciate it. Now I put on some music, sat in the dining room away from the distraction of all the other books, and read the words closely. Kalman details the universal things that women hold, from family, love, and memories to food and objects. When I finished, I went back to the beginning, marveling at how this tiny little book could say so much.

I looked up at Ane, one of many women in the world holding things, and played Courtney Barnett's recent cover of the song "I'll Be Your Mirror" on my record player. Courtney Barnett was a new name to me, a young Australian singer, with vocals so pure it sounded like she was in my dining room, holding her guitar. She carried Nico's haunting femininity from the original 1967 version and gave it her own modern twist on The Velvet Underground tribute album released in September. I ordered the album a few months earlier and this was the first time I played it. Like the photograph and the Kalman book, it took me time to get there. The words rang as true as they had fourteen years earlier, but now Rich and I had added three more people to the mirror.

I'll be your mirror
Reflect what you are, in case you don't know
I'll be the wind, the rain and the sunset
The light on your door to show that you're home
When you think the night has seen your mind
That inside you're twisted and unkind
Let me stand to show that you are blind
Please put down your hands
'Cause I see you

With impatience, determination, and efficiency, Eliza also purchased her own one-of-a-kind pandemic portrait. She is not one to spend her allowance, and since her purchase of the minifridge back in June, she had managed to accrue enough money to buy this coveted item without our assistance. Rich and I tried to dissuade her. We suggested she take a bit more time to consider, maybe shop around for comparisons, but she argued that she might miss her chance or the price could go up. Putting me to shame, Eliza took no more than a week to discover, purchase, and finally display her beloved portrait in our home. It arrived framed and ready to go. Inspired by "Ane"'s spot in the dining room, Eliza removed a stretched canvas from our kitchen wall, an admittedly sappy, feel-good saying about family and home that had hung there for six years, and dropped it off on my freshly organized office bookshelf.

"I think this goes here," she said, placing it on the shelf before asking me to cover my eyes and leading me into the kitchen.

"Keep them closed. Okay closer. One more step. You can open them!" I turned to face the photograph, delighted, confused, and amazed by what this pandemic had brought into our home. An autographed, framed photo of Bob Saget, a.k.a. Danny Tanner, now watched over our kitchen with a toddler Michelle in his arms. Bob Saget had died a couple weeks earlier, lending a sense of urgency to this acquisition.

While not intending to be contradictory, Eliza balanced out our home with this photo of a man holding something. I was willing to embrace it, given the whole premise of *Full House* and its *Fuller House* reboot is that the three men are shouldering the burdens usually held by women. The show always annoyed me when I was younger, but it does challenge gender norms and paint a portrait of an imperfect family. Ian and Eliza loved watching old episodes, and it's thanks to a guest appearance that they occasionally asked me to play Macy Gray's music. *It's not that bad,* I thought, as Eliza beamed with pride and I fought back my laughter.

I even got used to the theme song, sometimes humming it during my daily kitchen encounters with Danny and Michelle. They were there with me as I started the coffee, took out the garbage, and got ready to walk the dog once again. While I would not have put the track on my pandemic album, the message was not so different from "I'll Be Your Mirror" or Maira Kalman's book. *"When you're lost out there and you're all alone, a light is waiting to carry you home."*

Despite all the difficulties we have held over the course of these couple years, our home was full of love and we surrounded ourselves with music and laughter. Music is my light. Thank you.

BONUS TRACKS

These two essays serve as additions to *Soundtrack: Liner Notes from a Pandemic Mixtape*. I started "Leaving New York" in 2019, prior to the pandemic, and finished it during the summer of 2020. It was published under the title "Reflections on 9/11 and Leaving New York." Honoring the memory of 9/11 in the context of covid provided space and time to consider the impact of both tragedies, and it drove me to research the stories and recall very specific details from nearly twenty years earlier. Similarly, the story I tell in "You Don't Know Me" is directly connected to my pandemic writing process, and in a way provides an ending to the collection. In this essay, a series of interconnected events and the work of another author helped me discover why I write these stories.

BONUS TRACK I

Leaving New York

New York City is a love story. It is beauty, pain, concrete and air with millions of little lives colliding and crisscrossing into one giant ecosystem. It transcends explanation but we know its energy when we feel it and it is unmistakably New York. In our twenties, brunches led to exploring Chelsea galleries, record stores on St. Marks Place, bowling at Bowlmor and *moules frites* at Felix. Later we traded middle-of-the-night diners for middle-of-the-night feedings, with New York the backdrop to our changing, shifting, evolving lives.

When I realized my post-college fling with New York might be more permanent, I left jobs in fashion and at start-ups to become a teacher. One day, while teaching second graders to tell time on an analog clock, one student, wise beyond his years, commented, "Each second that passes, each minute—that's the only time it will be that exact time. Like today is March 3, 2011, at 10:15 in the morning, and

I don't know how many seconds. See? It keeps changing. You can only live each second once."

A picture flashed in front of me from a decade earlier, a second, an instant, that we New Yorkers relive again and again. We may only live through the reality of the day once, but the stories that unfolded with the crumbling towers, the way it changes and shifts each year in our memories, how we carry it with us lives on. New York is a city that went to bed that night below clouds of smoke and woke the next day to show us that time would march forward, no matter how hard we tried to press rewind.

When I drive down the West Side Highway now, I always slow down as I approach Chelsea and look out the window to my left, anticipating that giant red-brick warehouse-style building on West 26th Street, with balconies overlooking the Hudson River and downtown Manhattan. It doesn't matter how many happy hours we had or how many lunch breaks we enjoyed outside on that balcony. What I remember, what I see most clearly, is that September morning.

In 2001, my usual walk to work at a small start-up took me from the subway station at 23rd Street and 8th Avenue to 26th and 12th, where the landmark Starrett-Lehigh building occupies an entire city block. Designers, photographers, and filmmakers rode the freight elevator with us, exiting at various floors where their creative work emerged from the canvases of giant, many-paned windows and sweeping city views. On September 11, the sky was crystal clear. I don't need to rely on my own memory for this: it was all over the reports that day, both before and after.

At a Catholic elementary school on West 25th street, a security officer and I shared a smile, recognizing each other from our morning routines. "Nice day," he commented. What happened to his day after that? Did children at that school lose parents? Did he lose friends or colleagues? Could the Catholic priests and nuns lessen the pain or help make sense of this? I'll never know the answers. It was around eight a.m. and there were kids playing outside and he was watching them jump rope and play hopscotch, keeping them safe as their parents said goodbye. He was smiling in the sun on a New York City morning.

The next couple hours are slow motion, and this is my version of a story told millions of times. Where were you on 9/11 when the Twin Towers fell? I was at my desk at work at a start-up called SportsCapsule. Despite much of New York culture arriving at work between nine and ten a.m., we all arrived early. Each of us sat quietly at our own desk, spaced-out in an open-plan, warehouse-style office. Our flip-flopped feet rested on cement floors beneath Aeron chairs as we stared at our computer screens, drank coffee, and checked e-mails.

Suddenly we were all there together, looking out those painfully large, south-facing windows. Then we went to the balcony. Then we were not sure we should be on the balcony. Then we were on AOL instant messenger—AIM for short. Then we were getting phone calls. Then we couldn't get phone calls. Then we were trying to get news updates. Then we went to the bathroom. Then we felt like we might throw up. Then we were back at our desks. Then we didn't know what to do. Then we left the office. The streets were quiet except for a few men in camouflage with machine guns standing on the corner, and we became aware for the first time that the Starrett-Lehigh's basement tenant was the FBI.

My boss considered leaving her car in the garage where she always parked it, but the streets were empty, so she drove. She drove my friend Alex and me north along 12th Avenue and dropped us near

Alex's Hell's Kitchen apartment. We saw someone in medical scrubs and asked where we should go to give blood. Roosevelt Hospital? The person gave us a grave look and said they already have more than they need. With six packs of beers from a corner deli, we went to Alex's apartment, to the outdoor deck where we had gathered for birthdays, engagements, music, and memories. The crowd grew as friends found their way from various parts of Manhattan. I got a text from Laura, my friend from high school in Toronto who had been living in New York for all of six days at that point. In the age of flip phones and short messages, she told me she was okay. We made a plan to meet at her new apartment the following day.

A day or two later, only minutes after Laura and I passed Michael Douglas and Catherine Zeta-Jones walking slowly, pushing their child in a stroller through Central Park, I saw an old college friend running. "Eric!" I called, and he turned to see the look on my face that said, "You're alive!" He answered, "I'm okay. I don't work at Cantor anymore." The pain in his eyes revealed lost friends and a deep knowledge that with one different decision, it could have been him. The sought-after path of Cornell graduate to Cantor Fitzgerald associate was a coveted one until it wasn't.

We gathered news of tragedies. Neil was a young computer programmer at a company where I worked before SportsCapsule. I only had the chance to know him briefly but now I'd remember him forever. Neil spent a recruiting event telling our college recruits about his fiancée, his family, and how he loved his New York life between his turns on the bowling lane. His gratitude and happiness sold those kids on their own futures. Neil and some other former colleagues of mine were on a team of consultants staffed at Cantor. He went to work early that day.

One of my best friends from college, Moira, was living in San Francisco during 9/11, but her Uncle Eamon was killed. He spent his career at Cantor Fitzgerald and rescued many people from the World Trade Center bombing in 1993. ESPN made a documentary about him. Just when I thought my friends in other cities were safe, the ripples of the damage reverberated around us, leaving the gravity of what we had witnessed and an acute sense of our own mortality to sink in. Each moment is its own. We will never live it again.

Every year, the anniversary is marked by something different, some other memory, a mix of sadness, nostalgia, loss, gratitude, and hope that almost seems to define the word anniversary. On September 10, 2002, I went on my first "date" with my now husband, Rich. We went to see a band play with my friend Adeeb. They sang a cover of "Bring On the Dancing Horses" by Echo & the Bunnymen. As our other friends parted over the course of the night, Rich and I ended up sharing late-night falafel on a stoop in the East Village and singing "New York State of Mind" in a basement karaoke joint. A week earlier, we barely knew each other. Suddenly, we were moving through the city together as the clocks struck midnight and it was, once again, September 11.

A couple months later, for my twenty-sixth birthday, my aunt took me shopping in Soho. I picked out a coat, the most expensive piece of clothing I'd ever owned. It was a brown wool knee-length coat by Rebecca Taylor, with a delicate floral trim and lining. The chocolate color matched my hair, and the double-breasted buttons were more narrow than usual, softening the silhouette. I remember looking at myself in the mirror, still on cloud nine with this new boyfriend, and thinking, "Life's too short."

The sixth anniversary, 2007, was a Tuesday again like the first time. A few days earlier, I welcomed my third-grade students to a new school year at Little Red in the West Village. It was my first year as a head teacher. The father of one of my students Sal was a firefighter killed in 9/11. Sal was three years old and his brother Vincent a baby when their father died. On 9/11 Sal shared a medal with the class, along with a letter sent to his family from President Bush. Tears welled up in my eyes as Sal read the letter, his voice steady and proud. It didn't seem fair that at nine years old Sal had processed enough grief to face this moment with poise.

On September 11, 2008, I was a new mother. That shifted my focus from Sal to his mother. That day. Her loss. Her grief. Holding young Vincent in her arms and listening as a neighbor told three-year-old Sal that he was now the man of the house. So many widows left to make sense of the senselessness, so many children without a parent. Holding a new life of my own, a one-month-old son named Robert, I realized how each life is held by many others, creating exponential loss.

Over the next few years, September 11 gradually became not only a day of tragedy but what it had been before that, my younger brother's birthday. Kevin was born on September 11, 1983. He was two months early, a middle-of-the-night emergency when my mother hemorrhaged from placenta previa. Neighbors cleaned up the blood while my dad rushed her to the hospital. Kevin suffered a stroke but survived. He was our September 11 miracle before the date had meaning.

Memories of lives lived emerged from the tragedy of those same lives lost. Legacies were honored, stories recorded and shared, and families continued on very different paths but they kept going. A writer I know wrote a story about a life she never envisioned with a man she would never have met, all because 9/11 took her first husband's life when she was twenty-seven years old.

Two children later, strollers and scooters filled the tiny foyer in our New York City apartment and in a postpartum whirlwind, we landed twenty miles away in Rye, New York. I came across an essay collection published around the time we moved called *Goodbye to All That: Writers on Loving and Leaving New York*, taking its title from Joan Didion's 1967 essay. The proximity of the city made our move less dramatic, but reading these essays, I could feel the reality sink in. We had left. In a search for love songs to the city, I found REM's "Leaving New York," released in 2004 but new to me. New York had been my home longer than any other place, and could have been home forever. I would—will—always love it.

I entered our new life with excitement and anticipation, but also with an unshakable feeling of loss. I thought I'd be leaving 9/11 behind, too, but instead, wove more threads in the fabric of its memory. A plaque at our local YMCA tells the story of a young man named Christopher who grew up in Rye, now twenty-five years old forever. My children's hockey coach lost his three close friends—Teddy, Tommy, and Ward—and presents a coaching award every year in their honor.

On the eighteenth anniversary, September 11, 2019, I woke up bleary-eyed and started writing, needing to preserve this story. Partway through writing with a busy day ahead, I clicked save. My kids went to school and I went to work, with little reminders interrupting the otherwise normal day.

Rob's youth soccer team played at halftime at the high school varsity soccer game that evening. Gazing at all these young people who never shared a day alive with the victims of 9/11, the power of time was palpable. I opened that day's *New York Post* while waiting for the game to start, an impulse purchase that morning at the deli. On the cover, it promised a list of names inside, and I was finally ready to find the ones I recognized. Eamon. Neil. Christopher. Sal's dad.

After the game and once my younger children were in bed, Rob and I sat down together to watch a movie he saw at school that day, *Man in Red Bandana*. His teacher showed it to them, wanting these students to know the legacy of his childhood friend, Welles, who was featured in the film. Then we watched the ESPN video about Moira's Uncle Eamon and I sent Moira a text to let her know I was thinking of her. Before going upstairs, I read Rob the first half of this essay I had written at five a.m. that morning.

When I sent Moira's text, I noticed a message from an unfamiliar number. It read, "Always thinking of SportsCapsule on 9/11. Hope you and yours are well." I tucked Rob into bed, then texted back to find out it was my old friend and colleague, Mark. We had slowly gone back to work at SportsCapsule a few days after the towers fell, but only to hear for certain that our start-up was winding down. Loading old desktop computers and office memorabilia into the trunks of taxicabs, we headed to our respective apartments to file for unemployment and figure out what came next. We kept in touch for a while, but by 2019 I hadn't talked to Mark in over a decade. Seeing his name in a text, I could hear his voice distinctly and picture his AIM name popping up in a bubble on my monitor as we exchanged silent jokes from a few feet away.

Putting my phone down, I clicked my computer on to return to this essay, but not before scrolling through back-to-school photos on Facebook. A post from my friend Glenn caught my attention. It was a picture of a young man named Swede, with a note about

Swede's character, their friendship, and his death on 9/11. I remembered Swede from college. I could picture him at parties, smiling and friendly. I didn't know him well and the memories are more like a watercolor than a photograph. In those eighteen years I had never realized Swede was among the victims, among the stories left for loved ones to keep alive. I went back to that newspaper and found two more names: Welles and Swede.

Making a mental note to take my kids to the 9/11 memorial soon, I reflected on the effect of time, and how events mark our lives with these phases and anniversaries and only as an adult do we see that life is more circular than it is linear. I thought about a day in the 1980s when my dad took us to visit the Vietnam Memorial in Washington, DC, when I was about nine or ten years old. My dad served in Vietnam in 1969, drafted right after he graduated college. I was born in 1976, only seven years later, the third of four children. By the time we went to visit the memorial, my dad had coached countless softball teams. We had built family memories from Fourth of July parades, Halloween trick-or-treating in the neighborhood, vacations and Christmases. His jokes, his love of vanilla milkshakes, his role as a great father and husband are what I remember.

There were not many stories about Vietnam. We were in DC for my sister's soccer tournament, and the memorial was a side trip. Yet when we arrived, the visit felt significant for my dad. I remember him finding the name of his close high school friend who died in the war before my dad even arrived on Vietnamese soil. When we are kids, we almost forget that there was any time before us, and as inertia moves us forward, these revealing moments are the ones that stand out, the clues to events that shaped our families and our world before we existed. That's how my children will learn about

9/11, and why writing down these memories felt so important.

On a last whim before shutting off the lights and heading to bed, I pulled an old college photo album down from the bookshelf. I could not let this eighteenth anniversary of 9/11 end without revisiting the night my New York City love story began. It was spring of 1998, my senior year of college. On a Saturday afternoon in May, after hatching a midnight plan the night before, four friends—Veronica, Dominique, Grant, and me—piled into my beat-up Jeep Cherokee and headed to Manhattan for a night out.

Our plan was to celebrate the friendships forged in those Ithaca hills before graduating and scattering to new cities. We had no reason to go to New York City that night, but no reason not to go either. After pulling through the Lincoln Tunnel, we headed south to a restaurant that Grant knew from the Hotel School and through family connections in the restaurant industry. He promised it would change our lives. We rode an elevator to the top of the World Trade Center and exchanged our giddiness for confidence as we entered the bar area, unable to secure or afford a table at the actual restaurant.

Nestled into a cozy booth with menus boasting The Greatest Bar on Earth, we ordered the cheapest bottle of champagne available, stretching our college budgets. Grant's father knew the chef, and I didn't think much of it when he asked our server to mention his dad's name. Could the chef stop by our table if he has a chance? Moments later we put down our champagne flutes to shake hands with the famous chef Michael Lomonaco, a man who a few years later survived the falling towers only to have his restaurant's event calendar replaced by weeks, maybe months of funerals for his friends and colleagues.

That night, we knew nothing of this fate as we asked strangers to take group photos, smiling ear to ear in the best downtown outfits we could cobble together from our closets upstate. As the bubbles of the champagne worked their magic, we went to the floor-to-ceiling windows across the bar and pressed our foreheads against the glass, gazing down on the city below. A window to the world. A glimpse into our future. A feeling that anything was possible.

Recently, I pulled the brown coat out of a basement closet, found the couple buttons that had fallen off from years of wear, and took it to a local tailor for repair. Those buttons, first one and then a second, remained in my jewelry box through many moves. Other than two buttons and a torn seam in the pocket, the coat was in fine condition. In the same way that memories can go to the back or the front of our mental closet, I returned the now-mended coat to my wardrobe, eager to weave that piece of who I used to be with who I am today. The floral trim flirts with the double-breasted shape, begging the coat and the woman wearing it not to take life too seriously.

Some sights and scents from 9/11 have disappeared from my memory. Nightmares faded long ago, and while I can still see the towers falling, my stomach doesn't rise in my throat in response. I cherish that coat and the old, grainy 35mm photos from Windows on the World, and somewhere I might even have a newspaper from that day. My September 11, 2019, *New York Post*—despite my intention to save it—must have found its way to the recycling bin. We don't always get to decide who and what we keep, but we hold on to the love stories.

BONUS TRACK 2

You Don't Know Me

7/17/2003
Hey Jeff,
Rock N Roll!!!
XO,
Danielle and R___

I don't know Jeff or Danielle and I cannot make out the third name in this inscription beyond the R, but I feel incredibly lucky that at some point between July 2003 and late August 2022, Jeff ran out of room on his shelf (though hopefully he continued rockin' and rollin') and this book, Nick Hornby's *Songbook*, found its way to me.

I loved this book so much that one day when I had to stop reading to go make dinner, I paused before putting it down and found myself smiling and staring at the cover. Although I stopped short of making an outward declaration, the words "You complete me" did cross my mind. For a spiritual agnostic like me, finding this book at the particular moment I found it made me wonder about the possibility of divine intervention. It was kismet at the very least. You don't find this kind of magic on Amazon.

Over the summer of 2022 I took particular delight in the hands-on, low-tech experience of in-person shopping, of going into a store and not knowing what I might find. The pleasure of unknown outcomes stood in stark contrast to the goal-orientation and overwhelming choices of online ordering, and to the covid-inspired trend of curbside pickup. It's why shopping at farmer's markets beats the grocery store routine. Not everything gets checked off the list, but that one loaf of zucchini bread is worth the extra stop, along with being outside and having conversations with people who love what they do.

My favorite store in any small town is the bookstore, the quirkier the better. Small bookstores have their own personalities and reflect the communities that sustain them. At age nine, Ian has developed a love of old stuff, and when he goes into a second-hand store, he investigates each item as if it is sunken treasure he pulled up from the bottom of the sea. He knows he is not allowed to take the whole chest of jewels home, and he is trying to find the one he will value the most (and whose actual value fits within his small spending allowance). It's the same feeling I have in independent bookstores—and in stores that sell used books and records, I get even more absorbed. Here, each item contains not only the written story or song list, but also the story of the person who touched it, bought it, read or listened to it, then parted ways with it to give it another life.

When my kids were very little, I passed Black Cat Books almost daily on our summer vacations on Shelter Island, but I was so busy parenting that I rarely found the time to go inside and look around. The store occupies a shingled two-story house set back from the main road with a little gravel parking lot out front. Its sign, no surprise, is a black cat, and there is always a shelf of marked down books outside the entrance. A short distance from the bank, the post office, and the island's only grocery store, Black Cat is in a prime location, but it is so unassuming that one could drive by many times with no idea of the possibilities within its walls.

Around 2016, I bought a record player and we started collecting vinyl. My friend Matthew mentioned that they have records at Black Cat, too, and my kids and I were thrilled to find they also have a wide range of children's books—perfect for summer reading. We started visiting regularly to look through the shelves, flip through the records, and sometimes trade in old books for credit towards new ones. I found time to stop by on my own, too, looking for inspiration or to shop for a gift. A friend of mine pointed out that part of the beauty of used bookstores is that the merchandising doesn't influence your choices in the same way it does in the dwindling number of big box stores or even independent bookstores. Publishers cannot push big displays of the hottest summer read if a store does not sell new books. In theory, this could make it harder to discern what might be good or not; in practice, I often find books I love.

On a quiet August day in the summer of 2022, my friend Emily and I took our sons to Black Cat Books. The familiar shelves of children's books are just inside the entrance, opposite a staircase leading to the second floor. Most of the store's collection is on the first floor, with fiction and non-fiction in the front room on floor-to-ceiling bookshelves and center tables. The records are neatly organized by genre in bins under the windows and a couch creates an inviting reading nook right in the middle of everything. Art, design, and rare books fill the shelves toward the back of the store where Michael, the owner, works at the register, the windows around him giving glimpses of a backyard garden perfect for reading. Much of Black Cat's business is online sales of rare books, and Michael is often multi-tasking between wrapping those books for shipment while making recommendations and small talk with his in-person customers. He never tries to sell me anything, yet something about the place makes me want to buy nearly everything.

That summer Ian got into manga, the Japanese comics and graphic novels that have recently become wildly popular among American kids. We asked Michael if he had any manga, and of course the answer was yes, upstairs in the room next to the office. In all these years I had never been upstairs. The arrow leading upstairs says "Music Books," and for some reason, rather than realizing this could be the perfect combination of my two favorite things, I must have thought it was books of sheet music (I am not a musician) and never climbed the short flight to find out.

Up we went, the boys leading the way. As they sat cross-legged on the floor in front of the manga and other graphic novels, I stood in the hall, scanning the shelves of music books—biographies of musicians, books by musicians, and countless books on music history and criticism covering all genres. I found one called *The Rap Year Book: The Most Important Rap Song From Every Year Since 1979, Discussed, Debated, and Deconstructed,* and held it close under one arm. It was the perfect belated fourteenth birthday gift for Rob. Right at eye level I saw a small hardcover, the scrawl on its spine reminiscent of teen handwriting. *Nick Hornby. Songbook.*

Pulling it from the shelf, I felt an immediate connection to it. I opened it and saw the inscription to Jeff and the CD inside the back cover. A lot changes in two decades. *How would I listen to this CD?* I thought. The cover had song titles scribbled on it and a couple drawings of little characters, along with a coffee mug ring whose origin was difficult to trace. Was it part of the design, or had Jeff placed his coffee on it one day?

I'd read a bunch of Nick Hornby books in my 20's. I loved them. I loved him. I loved the movies they became. When Rich and I first met, we sized each other up in a flirtatious manner by answering the famous *High Fidelity* question, "Top five albums of all time." Rich was decisive with Led Zeppelin, Pink Floyd's *The Wall*, and Bob Marley on his list. Mine included The Velvet Underground, Sinéad O'Connor, and probably *The Queen Is Dead* by The Smiths. I think we found common ground with U2's *The Joshua Tree*. I remember not being able to narrow down to fill that fifth slot, wanting to leave room for the future. I was only twenty-five, after all.

But I had never come across *Songbook*, at Black Cat or elsewhere. It wasn't downstairs in the fiction or memoir sections where *High Fidelity*, *Fever Pitch* and *About a Boy* were likely sitting, ready to be reborn. It was nestled up here among the music books, because it is a book about thirty-one songs that influenced Hornby's life and writing. The book paints a self-portrait, mosaic-like, with various beautiful fragments from other artists. I had never seen anything like *Songbook*—except that I had: in the many drafts of a manuscript I had spent the past two years writing. I tried to be present with Ian and our friends as I walked back to the manga section with this secret talisman tucked under my arm. I couldn't believe the book had left Jeff's home and withstood the curiosity of other customers so that it was sitting here, waiting for me, bringing a sprinkle of enchantment to an otherwise typical summer day.

Songbook came to me at a pivotal moment. I had recently completed the manuscript for this book. After editing, re-reading, and sharing it with a few friends, the project felt finished. I wanted it published—polished, completed, bound—but didn't know how best to make that happen. So before heading out to Shelter Island, I'd printed a copy at Staples and mailed it to my 102-year-old grandmother, then wrote a cover letter and emailed it off to an editor.

In that moment of vulnerability while waiting to hear back, I began to wonder why I had worked so hard on this book for so long. It had started as a few journal entries in March 2020 when the pandemic began, and as covid lingered on, the essays just kept growing. *What if no one likes it? What if I wasted two years? What if it just isn't good?* Then I found *Songbook*, and it all made sense. I'd felt compelled to write the essays in this book as the events around me unfolded. Digging into history and pieces of my past had helped me gain perspective on the frightening, precarious present. I worked and reworked the essays because I cared about them and wanted to practice the craft of writing. Hopefully my kids and the rest of my family would one day read the book. If a few hundred other people did, too, that would mean the world to me. Nick Hornby didn't write *Songbook* to be a huge commercial success, or to sell the film rights. He wrote it because it mattered to him. And now, it mattered to me, more than he could have imagined, probably more than it had mattered to Jeff, but who knows? Maybe Jeff had a moment like this and outgrew it, creating the possibility for me to savor it now.

Nick Hornby was forty-four and a father of two kids when he started writing *Songbook* in 2001. I was forty-three when I started writing my book and forty-five when I finished. When I read all those Hornby books in my twenties, before marriage and kids and life, I drank them in, but may not have fully appreciated the complexities. In *Songbook*, I understood Hornby and his writing in a new way.

I had a solo bus ride to read the last half, and a night alone in my house to listen to tracks from the book—on YouTube rather than the CD. I'd forgotten how much I liked Ben Folds Five back in '98. In his essay, Hornby describes their amusing song "Kate" so perfectly—a teenager's crush progresses from an infatuation with the multitalented Kate to realizing she sleeps and breathes like everyone else. I remembered that Ben Folds, now performing solo, was coming to The Capitol Theatre in the next town over sometime soon. *Help me, Google, when?* August 31! Five days away. Tickets still available. Before I knew what was happening, I was dancing in my living room.

For the next few days, I carried the book with me everywhere like a security blanket, a reminder that this feeling of connection is why we write. It's why we read. It's what makes bookstores magical and music viscerally memorable. Nothing had changed, yet everything felt different.

The next week, I took Ian and his friend to the Ben Folds concert. We listened to a recent setlist to prepare, and I was struck by the humor and accessibility of the songs. Ian especially loved "Effington" and "Rock This Bitch," for obvious reasons. The music was so engaging it was hard to believe it was a lone person up there with only a piano and a microphone. Between songs, Ben Folds was funny and endearing, and he even invited audience participation on the hit song "You Don't Know Me," giving us the responsibility of singing Regina Spektor's part. He played "Kate." He played "Army." And he played a bunch of other songs that I hadn't known and now love. All because Jeff decided he was done with *Songbook*.

But I wasn't quite done. It felt like Michael at Black Cat Books should know what he'd given me—this spell of a just-right book at a just-right moment. Back on Shelter Island for Labor Day weekend,

I dropped Ian and Eliza at the library and, for possibly the first time in my history of book-buying, I went back to the bookstore to say, *Thank you so much for this book. I loved it.*

My thank-you to Michael led down another path of overlapping friends, shared musical interests, and a lively conversation with another customer, Tom, who happened to be hosting a discussion about music at the library that evening. I would soon realize that, though I had never met him before, Tom* was already a piece of my story, but we didn't know that yet as the three of us stood talking. I explained why Hornby's book meant so much to me—because I'd been writing a bunch of essays as a soundtrack, and I used to assume a lot of people organized their lives according to music, and who knows if they do or not, but Nick Hornby does, and for that I was grateful. I think I used the word "validating," and I meant it.

Tom and Michael know a lot about literature, music, and writing, and if I ever host a podcast like the BBC's *Desert Island Discs*, I will definitely interview them. We talked about famous rock stars and Shelter Island musicians. We talked about small venues, outdoor venues, CBGBs, and the first Lollapalooza. We talked until a family came up to the register, not wanting to interrupt but hoping to actually purchase some books. The dad approached the counter and put his pile of books down, with *About a Boy* right on top. Nick Hornby again. Call it coincidence, a small world, magic, or fate. Or maybe just call it a bookstore.

*Tom is Tom Junod, the journalist who inspired Lloyd Vogel's character in *A Beautiful Day in the Neighborhood*. This essay brought me full circle, back to Track 1.

ACKNOWLEDGMENTS

Is that all there is? Then let's keep dancing.

—PJ Harvey

t has been such an adventure to write these essays and to fix these memories in space and time. I've learned about women I admire and women who have shaped my life, investigating their words and their stories as I put my own down on paper. Of course, I didn't stick with female musicians, and the essays veered in many different directions, but the essence remained.

Only a few days before this book was scheduled to print, I got a text from my friend Allison (Double L). Sinéad O'Connor died. Standing in the hallway of the 18th-century house where I work, I felt the stability of the wide floorboards beneath my feet and stared, squinting at my phone to maybe make the words disappear. In a breath, I moved from disbelief to understanding. I could never have written *Soundtrack* without Sinéad's music. As I add these final paragraphs to a project I've worked on for over three years, I am shocked and sad and missing her.

When David Bowie died, this quote went viral: "If you're sad today, just remember the world is over four billion years old and you somehow managed to exist at the same time as David Bowie." That's how I feel about Sinéad O'Connor (and David Bowie, but he's not in this book). I got ready for work on July 26 with her music playing throughout my house, and returned to find it still playing; in that way, she is still alive. She gave the world her beautiful voice, an eternal gift. I wish our collective love and admiration had lessened Sinéad's lifelong struggles and eased the unbearable pain she felt after her 17-year-old son Shane died in January 2022. I wish we could have helped her the way she helped so many of us. In her honor, we can speak up on issues that matter, be more compassionate, and fill our lives with music. I think Sinéad would like that as her legacy.

During the time I was writing these essays, Sinéad wrote an auto-biography, her own deep dive into family, religion, music, and finding her voice. Chrissie Hynde released a solo album called *Standing in the Doorway: Chrissie Hynde Sings Bob Dylan*. Patti Smith canceled a world tour and stayed in New York, and lived like most of us did, taking care of herself and binge-watching television, in her case *Law & Order*. Something tells me she probably wrote a few books during the solitude. My friend Hanadi and I saw Patti take the stage again in February 2022, right down the road at The Capitol Theatre.

Dolores O'Riordan lives on through her music. On those endless Spotify mixes, I discovered The Cranberries' covers of Fleetwood Mac's "Go Your Own Way" and the Christmas classic, "Little Drummer Boy." I recently watched *Derry Girls* with Ian and heard their songs set against the perfect backdrop: '90s Ireland.

Tom Hanks released a new movie. Of course he did. It's called *Finch*, and apparently it was a huge success but I have yet to see it. He also released a World War II miniseries. But my most recent memory of Tom Hanks is listening to his interview on *Desert Island Discs* on a ride back from Pennsylvania with Rob. I also saw a drawing of Mr. Hanks while visiting my college friend Tasha in Newburyport, Massachusetts. She had a thank-you note on display, a sketch of Tom Hanks' smiling face in red with T.HANKS next to it in block letters. I wonder where he'll show up next.

While all those people were doing their thing in the big world, a lot of people were doing things in my little world for which I will be forever grateful.

To my writing group—Amy, Ann, Aviva, Emi, Jackie, Jamie, Margot, Paula, Sonali—thank you for showing up every week, for listening, for sharing, for encouraging, for tissues, and for genuine friendship. There is a beautiful Sinéad song called "Thank You for Hearing Me." That one is for you. Your support means the world to me. It is incredible to think we made it through these couple years, still meeting nearly every week, even when it had to be in a Brady Bunch-like configuration on a Zoom screen.

Mom, where would we be without you? You taught us about love with all its imperfections. You always made room for stories, from re-telling hazy dreams over a cup of tea in the morning hours to long phone conversations. A mother who listens might be the best gift there is in this world.

To my sister Chrissy, I entered the world with a best friend. You have been with me every day, even though you are on the other side of the world. To my bonus sisters, Laurel and Alexa, thank you for always including me. I wish we could listen to one more song all together.

To my grandmothers, Gigi who is still alive and Grandma Cupp, your strength paved the way for generations of women to follow.

Gigi, I am so glad to have had some special moments with you over the past two years and that we found a way to bond over our love of books. Aunt Donna, as my mom's sister, you hold a special place in our family and I can't wait to see you again.

Caroline and Deb, you have both been role models for me as long as I've known you, leading your lives with conviction and compassion. Thank you for loving my brothers.

Speaking of love and brothers, I have some pretty great men in my life, too. Dad, Sam, and Kevin—you are all the perfect blend of support and humor. Thank you for making me laugh through all the years. Rich, your loyalty and unconditional love means the world to me. You are my mirror, just as you promised to be over fifteen years ago. And through you, I have become part of a second family with your parents, Charlotte and Adam.

Wylie, thank you for believing in me and in this project. You dedicated countless hours to helping me fine-tune these essays, and I couldn't ask for a better editor. The fact that you are also one of my favorite people made it extra special.

Allison (Double L), I have admired your style since we first met when our kids were in kindergarten. 1976 Al(l)isons have an enduring bond, and from my early messy drafts, you translated my words into art. It's a bonus that we share taste in music and had a chance to celebrate at Regina Spektor's concert.

Myles and the team at Mascot Books, you were enthusiastic, thoughtful, diligent, and patient. You moved me along with the care and expertise I needed to make this book happen.

Friendships are hard to measure, and so many people who matter to me may not see themselves on the pages or in this list, yet you are here. We are all part of each other's history and future; we are on each other's soundtracks. Thank you to Jessica, Stephanie, and my friends from Malvern who are too many to list, and to Laura in Toronto who took me in when I was new and alone and needed a friend. Nancy, thank you for your openness and welcoming me back into your life, proving that people can pick up where they left off, even with decades in between.

To the friends who lifted me up throughout the pandemic, I hope I did the same for you. Susannah, Meredith, Nina, Pam, Maria, Leah, Maneli, Nuala, Lesley, Veronica, Katie, Moira, Melissa, Rebecca, Rachel, Kelli and Jen, I knew I could turn to any of you any time and find an open ear on the other end of the phone. Emily, having you by my side for over twenty-five years has been an immeasurable gift. Karen, you were the first adult I hugged other than Rich in those early months, and I am forever grateful for the deep friendship we built. Anna, thank you for being one of the best listeners and greatest advocates. Rebecca, those long walks through Mashomack with you were such a bright spot in the pandemic, and I can't wait to walk miles with you again. Jenny (and Matthew), thank you for sending me that article in March 2020. I miss seeing you and sharing stories. Drew, Steve, KC, Chris, Glenn, and my many high school and college friends, you are always up for a phone call, a visit, or a walk down memory lane.

To our Shelter Island crew, Rich and I are so lucky we have you at our home away from home. I can't help but smile when I ride that ferry, knowing I'm about to see you. To my Rye book club, thank you for continuing to meet and talk (a little bit) about books, except when we need to have a circle of trust instead. Amanda, Danielle, Genevieve, and Molly, that text chain we started in February 2020 kept me laughing and was the best reality check, even on the hardest days. Countless women in Rye brightened these days and years, from Erika, Emma, Sian, Tori, Vanessa, and our many neighborhood friends to Sheri, Gretchen, and Debbie at the Rye Historical Society. Jake and Christine, thank you for digging through the past with me.

I am fortunate to have writers and early readers who have kept pushing me forward. Monique, you inspire me and challenge me to work at it a little bit each day. Ann, you always make space at your table for a writing session on Little Ram Island. Serena, your insights, feedback, and our walks together gave me clarity. Sarah, thank you for your generosity in trading manuscripts. We have come a long way since we first met in Maureen's writing class at the Rye Arts Center. Nicole, Binders brought us back together, and what a gift it is to read your writing. Tom and Michael, thank you for the conversation at Black Cat Books. It was exactly what I needed to bring this project to completion.

Maybe a hundred years from now, someone will wonder what life was like during this time and these essays will serve as some sort of artifact. Maybe it will prompt someone to write more stuff down, to capture their own everyday moments, or to listen to more music. Whatever the outcome may be, this was worth it.

MUSIC ACKNOWLEDGMENTS

ABOUT THE AUTHOR

Alison Cupp Relyea is a writer and educator. She works at the Rye Historical Society and loves history almost as much as she loves music. She lives in Rye, New York, with her husband and three children.